( ) human rights *first*

The Constitution Project ★★★★★ ★ ★ ★

Habeas Works

Federal Courts' Proven Capacity to Handle Guantánamo Cases

A Report from Former Federal Judges

June 2010

About Human Rights First

Human Rights First believes that building respect for human rights and the rule of law will help ensure the dignity to which every individual is entitled and will stem tyranny, extremism, intolerance, and violence.

Human Rights First protects people at risk: refugees who flee persecution, victims of crimes against humanity or other mass human rights violations, victims of discrimination, those whose rights are eroded in the name of national security, and human rights advocates who are targeted for defending the rights of others. These groups are often the first victims of societal instability and breakdown; their treatment is a harbinger of wider-scale repression. Human Rights First works to prevent violations against these groups and to seek justice and accountability for violations against them.

Human Rights First is practical and effective. We advocate for change at the highest levels of national and international policymaking. We seek justice through the courts. We raise awareness and understanding through the media. We build coalitions among those with divergent views. And we mobilize people to act.

Human Rights First is a non-profit, non-partisan international human rights organization based in New York and Washington D.C. To maintain our independence, we accept no government funding.

Acknowledgements

Human Rights First would like to thank the following foundations for their generous support for this report:

Atlantic Philanthropies; John Merck Fund; Open Society Institute; Overbrook Foundation; Paul D. Schurgot Foundation

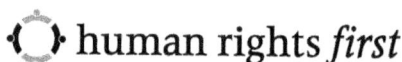

{ } human rights *first*

Headquarters

333 Seventh Avenue
13th Floor
New York, NY 10001-5108

Tel.: 212.845.5200
Fax: 212.845.5299

www.humanrightsfirst.org

Washington D.C. Office

100 Maryland Avenue, NE
Suite 500
Washington, DC 20002-5625

Tel: 202.547.5692
Fax: 202.543.5999

About the Constitution Project

The Constitution Project was founded in 1997 to create a climate for bipartisanship in defense of constitutional rights and values.

These rights and values include individual freedom, the presumption that those accused of crimes are innocent until proven guilty, greater transparency, accountability, and inclusiveness in government, and respect for the rule of law.

On each of the issues we address, the Project assembles a bipartisan coalition of respected leaders who create consensus recommendations for policy reforms. Working with these influential and unlikely allies, the Project conducts strategic public education campaigns and helps create the political majorities needed to transform this consensus into sound public policy.

Partner organizations and individuals rely on us to demonstrate that the policies we mutually advocate have broad bipartisan policy support, and we are a primary resource for the media when they explore whether bipartisan support exists and seek to identify unlikely allies who advocate for the policy reforms we address.

The Constitution Project is a non-partisan, non-profit think tank based in Washington D.C.

Acknowledgements

The Constitution Project would like to thank the following foundations for their generous support for this report:

Atlantic Philanthropies; Community Foundation for the National Capitol Region; CS Fund/Warsh-Mott Legacy; Foundation to Promote Open Society; Lawrence and Lillian Solomon Fund; Overbrook Foundation; Rockefeller Brothers Fund; Wallace Global Fund

The
Constitution Project
★★★★★★★

1200 18th Street, NW
Suite 1000
Washington, DC 20036

Tel: 202-580-6920
Fax: 202-580-6929

www.constitutionproject.org

This report is available for free online at www.constitutionproject.org and www.humanrightsfirst.org.

The following former federal judges endorse this report:

Hon. John J. Gibbons Appointed to the United States Court of Appeals for the Third Circuit by President Nixon; served 1970-1990

Hon. Shirley Hufstedler Appointed to the United States Court of Appeals for the Ninth Circuit by President Johnson; served 1968-1979

Hon. Nathaniel R. Jones Appointed to the United States Court of Appeals for the Sixth Circuit by President Carter; served 1979-2002

Hon. Thomas D. Lambros Appointed to the United States District Court, Northern District of Ohio, by President Johnson; served 1967-1995

Hon. Timothy K. Lewis Appointed to the United States District Court, Western District of Pennsylvania, by President George H.W. Bush; served 1991-1992; appointed to the United States Court of Appeals for the Third Circuit by President George H.W. Bush; served 1992-1999

Hon. James K. Logan Appointed to the United States Court of Appeals for the Tenth Circuit by President Carter; served 1977-1998

Hon. Abner Mikva Appointed to the United States Court of Appeals for the District of Columbia Circuit by President Carter; served 1979-1994

Hon. Robert P. Murrian Appointed United States Magistrate Judge to the United States District Court by the Judges of the Eastern District of Tennessee; served 1978-2002

Hon. William A. Norris Appointed to the United States Court of Appeals for the Ninth Circuit by President Carter; served 1980-1997

Hon. Robert O'Conor, Jr. Appointed to the United States District Court, Southern District of Texas, by President Ford; served 1975-1984

Hon. Stephen Orlofsky Appointed to the United States District Court, District of New Jersey, by President Clinton; served 1995-2003

Hon. Raul A. Ramirez Appointed to the United States District Court, Eastern District of California, by President Carter; served 1980-1989

Hon. Charles B. Renfrew Appointed to the United States District Court, Northern District of California, by President Nixon; served 1972-1980

Hon. H. Lee Sarokin Appointed to the United States District Court, District of New Jersey, by President Carter, served 1979-1994; appointed to the United States Court of Appeals for the Third Circuit by President Clinton; served 1994-1996

Hon. William S. Sessions Appointed to the United States District Court, Western District of Texas, by President Ford; served 1974-1987

Hon. Alfred M. Wolin Appointed to the United States District Court, District of New Jersey, by President Reagan; served 1987-2004

Contents

I. Executive Summary

Habeas is working. The judges of the U.S. District Court for the District of Columbia have ably responded to the Supreme Court's call to review the detention of individuals at Guantánamo Bay, Cuba. As former federal judges, many of us expressed our confidence as *amici* in *Boumediene v. Bush*[1] that courts are competent to resolve these cases.[2] We write now to affirm that our confidence has been vindicated. While we take no position on particular cases, a review of the District Court's treatment of the Guantánamo litigation convinces us that the court has effectively developed a consistent, coherent, and stable jurisprudence.

The government began to detain individuals at Guantánamo in January 2002. After a series of storied decisions culminating in *Boumediene v. Bush*, the Supreme Court charged the judges of the District Court with developing the framework for reviewing the habeas cases of individuals detained at Guantánamo in order to determine whether their detentions are lawful. Some commentators, including some judges and legislators, have suggested that the courts are struggling to take on an essentially legislative project, and that the courts are in desperate need of further instruction from Congress. On the contrary, courts are well suited to meet this challenge. Their competence in developing evidentiary and procedural rules comes from hard-won experience. District Court judges are on the front lines, applying the law to complex facts and balancing the competing needs of litigants. Because of their institutional competence, courts have historically developed rules of procedure and evidence. This was true under the common law, and is true of the Federal Rules.

In their "time-honored and constitutionally mandated roles of reviewing and resolving [habeas] claims,"[3] courts are also uniquely competent to determine the lawfulness of a prisoner's detention. In Guantánamo cases, courts make this determination by assessing whether the detention standard advanced by the government comports with the law, and then applying the standard to the particular facts of the case presented by a prisoner's habeas petition. Assessing the law, and applying it to facts. This is the core of what courts do. This is judging.

It comes as no surprise, then, that the District Court has capably answered the Supreme Court's charge. The bench has moved judiciously and cautiously to apply the pertinent law and develop the procedural rules governing habeas cases. In that way, the courts have gradually forged an effective jurisprudence that seeks to address the government's interest in national security while protecting the right of prisoners to fairly challenge their detention.

A. Detention Standard

In *Boumediene v. Bush*,[4] on remand from the Supreme Court, Judge Richard Leon adopted the detention standard used by the Department of Defense in Combatant Status Review Tribunals and endorsed by Congress. When the Obama Administration took office, the government modified the proposed detention standard based on the authority conferred by the Authorization for the Use of Military Forces (AUMF). Judge Reggie Walton adopted the new detention standard in *Gherebi v. Obama*,[5] under which the government claimed the right to detain individuals who "planned, authorized, committed, or aided" in the attacks of 9/11, or who "were part of, or substantially supported" the Taliban, al Qaeda, or associated forces.[6] The Administration conceded that its detention authority must comport with the Constitution and the law of war. Judge Walton found the government's standard met those requirements so long as "the terms 'substantially supported' and 'part of' are interpreted to encompass only individuals who were members of the enemy organization's armed forces."[7] In accordance with the principles of the common law, Judge Walton recognized that the contours of the standard would be developed as the standard was applied to the facts on a case-by-case basis. Subsequently, other judges of the District Court adopted and applied this standard.

The common law process has continued to refine the detention standard. In *Hamlily v. Obama*,[8] Judge John Bates agreed with Judge Walton's reasoning, but rejected "substantial support" as a basis of the government's detention authority.[9] The implication of this rejection is modest: While it produced a superficial divergence in the language used by the two courts, the substantive standard was largely the same. What the *Gherebi* standard accomplished by narrowly interpreting "substantial support," the *Hamlily* court did by rejecting "substantial support" as a basis for detention. Under both standards, the courts consider circumstantial evidence of membership, not just a petitioner's self-identification. Under both standards, the government must justify a prisoner's detention by demonstrating the prisoner was functionally a member of the Taliban, al Qaeda, or an associated force. Judge Bates recognized the functional equivalence of the two standards, asserting that any difference in the application of the standards "should not be great" because what qualifies as "substantial support" under *Gherebi* qualifies as "part of" under *Hamlily*.[10] Again, consistent with the tradition of the common law, other judges of the District Court have followed *Hamlily*, and found the standard "not inconsistent with Judge Walton's opinion in *Gherebi*."[11]

In *Al-Bihani v. Obama*,[12] involving an acknowledged member of a Taliban brigade, the U.S. Court of Appeals for the District of Columbia Circuit returned to the detention standard originally offered by the Bush Administration. The court also rejected the law of war as a constraint on the government's detention authority, contrary to the view of the Supreme Court in *Hamdi* and both the Bush and Obama Administrations. While we express no view on the D.C. Circuit's substantive opinion, we agree that the work of the U.S. District Court for the District of Columbia demonstrates that courts are competent to move carefully and incrementally in the application and refinement of a substantive detention standard. In the process, they have produced a body of law that provides a predictive framework for litigants and useful guidance for the government and intelligence agencies in the current military campaigns.

B. Procedural and Evidentiary Rules

The District Court has also developed effective rules of evidence and procedure that seek to balance the government's interest in protecting national security against the detainee's interest in his liberty. Shortly after the decision in *Boumediene*, Judge Thomas Hogan drafted a Case Management Order (CMO) to govern the Guantánamo litigation.[13] The result is a cautious and coherent set of procedural and evidentiary rules. The CMO established a model for the District Court, which has now applied the CMO to numerous cases, creating a common law interpreting its provisions. The government and detainees at Guantánamo look to these interpretations for guidance. What is more, the rules provide the essential flexibility required for addressing the new and complex factual scenarios presented by Guantánamo cases.

Boumediene established that prisoners at Guantánamo have a right to mount a meaningful challenge to their detention. The CMO protects that right by giving prisoners access to three categories of evidence: 1) exculpatory evidence; 2) evidence relied on by the government to justify its detention; and 3) additional evidence if and only if the detainee can show good cause. For the first category, the CMO directs the government to disclose to the petitioner "all reasonably available evidence in its possession that tends materially to undermine the information presented to support the government's justification for detaining the petitioner." Over a series of cases, the District Court has settled on the interpretation that "reasonably available" means information in one of three databases compiled by the government. The District Court judges have also arrived at uniform interpretations of what evidence "tends materially to undermine" the government's case. They agree, for instance, that it includes evidence that a witness was subjected to "abusive treatment [or] torture."[14]

The second category, evidence on which the government relies, includes "(1) any documents and objects in the government's possession that the government relies on to justify detention; (2) all statements, in whatever form, made or adopted by the petitioner that the government relies on to justify detention; and (3) information about the circumstances in which such statements of the petitioner were made or adopted."[15] The District Court judges interpret this language narrowly, and defer to assertions by the government that it did not rely on information requested by a detainee.

Under the CMO, disclosure of exculpatory evidence and evidence upon which the government relies is automatic. Disclosure of any additional evidence, however, requires a showing of good cause by the detainee. Such requests must be narrow and specific, must explain why the requested evidence is likely to show the prisoner's detention is unlawful, and must establish why production will not "unfairly disrupt [] or unduly burden [] the government."[16] The court is quick to reject broad requests and "fishing expeditions," but has granted narrow and

specific requests, such as requests for medical records and evidence of torture.

Beyond discovery, the courts have developed a host of procedural and evidentiary rules to assist in the orderly and judicious resolution of these cases, which evolve with experience. Foremost, the court has imposed a strict set of procedures that guard against the misuse or disclosure of classified evidence. On the merits, the courts have held the government must establish its case by a preponderance of the evidence—the standard proposed by the government. The government generally enjoys a rebuttable presumption that its evidence is authentic, but not that its evidence is accurate. Hearsay is admissible, with the weight given to a particular piece of hearsay determined by the court based on the entire record. Similarly, statements procured by torture or undue coercion are generally accorded no weight. The court designed these rules in an effort to avoid unduly burdening the government or compromising security, while still requiring it to justify the individual's detention.

C. The Results

Although the District Court has granted the writ of habeas corpus to 36 of the 50 individuals whose cases have reached final decisions, the raw numbers do not tell the whole story. One case in which the writ was granted involved 17 Uighurs, whom the government had already conceded were "no longer" enemy combatants and had agreed posed no threat to the United States.[17] Controlling for these 17 individuals, the government has prevailed in more than 40% of the habeas petitions that it has actually contested. Of the habeas cases that have reached resolution in the District Court, 18 appeals are pending, 12 by detainees and six by the United States. One of the cases on appeal, *Al Bihani v. Obama*, was affirmed, but the appellants are seeking *en banc* review.

Thus, a careful study of the D.C. federal courts' post-*Boumediene* jurisprudence shows that attacks on the judiciary's role are entirely unfounded. We fully recognize that Congress has the power, within constitutional limits, to set a detention standard of its own, and to prescribe rules of evidence and procedure to govern habeas cases. But in our considered judgment, reflecting our many years of experience on the bench, and based on our study of the available data, there is no need for Congress to do so here. Moreover, even if Congress were to legislate new standards, the courts will still have to interpret and apply the new law. Asking Congress to legislate an entirely new set of substantive or procedural rules to govern these cases would simply destabilize the emerging jurisprudence.

II. Introduction

After the Bush Administration decided to detain suspected terrorists at the military base at Guantánamo Bay, the judiciary faced a series of important questions about how these detainees might challenge the legality of their detention. In a series of incremental opinions, the Supreme Court confirmed that the detainees at Guantánamo Bay have the right to seek habeas corpus review of their detention in the federal courts. In making this important determination the Supreme Court intentionally left to the lower courts the project of refining the substantive and procedural standards to be used in these cases. Responding to this command, judges at the district court level have exercised their core competency and are steadily arriving at a consistent and careful jurisprudence.

We are a group of retired judges, most of whom joined an *amicus* brief in *Boumediene v. Bush*[18] in which we expressed confidence in the capacity of the judiciary to resolve these cases. This paper responds to recent critiques that express skepticism about the courts' ability to handle habeas cases brought by the detainees at Guantánamo Bay.[19] The goal of this paper is to dispel some of the myths that underlie those critiques and to demonstrate that the lower courts are succeeding in their delegated role. We hope to reassure Congress, the President, and the American public that judges are developing a careful and workable jurisprudence. As the courts continue to resolve these cases, they will build on a growing institutional expertise. We fully recognize that Congress has the power, within constitutional limits, to draft a new statute that would govern these cases. But our measured conclusion, based on the available data, is that such legislation would simply displace this emerging jurisprudence and require the courts to begin the process anew.

One point bears emphasis, and we will repeat it often in this paper. As former judges, we take no position on the particular outcomes of the habeas petitions or on the standards being developed in the court opinions. Some of us may have decided some cases differently. This much, however, is clear: the system is working. While Congress has the power to write a code that would govern these cases, legislation is not necessary and would disrupt the judiciary's successful development of coherent and consistent rules. Any new statute would require judicial interpretation that would guarantee years of additional litigation and re-introduce the uncertainty that the nation is finally putting behind us.

In the pages that follow, we provide a summary of the litigation culminating in the Supreme Court's decision in *Boumediene v. Bush*. We highlight the Supreme Court's intentional delegation of the common law process to the lower courts. We then discuss two District Court decisions as exemplars of the judicial process. Next, we address how the lower courts have succeeded in their constitutionally-contemplated role. In applying the substantive standard for detention, the courts are honing a coherent jurisprudence for post-9/11 habeas corpus cases. We discuss how it is a mischaracterization to describe the District Court judges as divided on the standard of detention. We then show how those judges have been equally successful in refining the procedural framework and evidentiary rules for these habeas corpus cases. In light of these successes, we conclude that the attacks on the competence of the judiciary are unfounded.

A. The Context of the Guantánamo Habeas Litigation

The Guantánamo habeas litigation has a long and eventful history. The first detainees arrived at the facility in January 2002. Originally, the Bush Administration planned to hold them with no legal process and no access to court or counsel. The first habeas petition, *Rasul v. Bush*, brought on behalf of two British nationals and one Australian, was filed February 19, 2002 in the District Court for the District of Columbia.[20] Not long after, *Rasul* was consolidated with similar litigation brought on behalf of a group of Kuwaiti prisoners.[21] In the summer of 2002, the government moved to dismiss the consolidated petitions. Relying on *Johnson v. Eisentrager*,[22] the government argued the detainees were beyond the jurisdiction of the federal courts. The District Court agreed, and the D.C. Circuit affirmed.[23] In November 2003, the Supreme Court granted *certiorari* to consider "the narrow but important question whether United States courts lack jurisdiction to consider challenges to the legality of the detention of foreign nationals captured abroad in connection with hostilities and incarcerated at the Guantánamo Bay Naval Base."[24]

The Supreme Court reversed, holding that the habeas statute, 28 U.S.C. § 2241 *et seq.*, conferred federal court jurisdiction. Writing for the majority, Justice Stevens noted that, unlike the petitioners in *Eisentrager*, the petitioners in *Rasul* and *Al Odah* (1) were not nationals of countries at war with the United States, (2) had "never been afforded access to any tribunal, much less charged with and convicted of wrongdoing" and (3) had "been imprisoned in territory over which the United States exercises exclusive jurisdiction and control."[25] In addition, the Court took note of the judiciary's long history of resolving habeas petitions. Courts had "exercised habeas jurisdiction over the claims of aliens detained within sovereign territory of the realm, as well as the claims of persons detained in the so-called 'exempt jurisdictions,' where

ordinary writs did not run, and all other dominions under the sovereign's control."[26]

Congress responded to *Rasul* by passing the Detainee Treatment Act of 2005 (DTA), which amended the habeas statute and purported to strip the federal courts of jurisdiction over habeas petitions filed by detainees at Guantánamo Bay.[27] In *Hamdan v. Rumsfeld*, however, the Court held that the DTA operated only prospectively, and had no application to habeas petitions filed before the effective date of the Act.[28] In response to *Hamdan*, Congress adopted the Military Commissions Act of 2006,[29] which removed any legislative ambiguity and stripped all federal courts of jurisdiction over any habeas petition brought by a detainee at Guantánamo, regardless of when it was filed, and limited detainees to the review process set up by the DTA.[30] This set up the historic questions addressed in *Boumediene v. Bush*: whether detainees at Guantánamo were guaranteed the right to habeas under the Constitution unless and until Congress suspended the writ, and if so, whether the review process provided by the DTA was an adequate substitute for habeas.

The Court answered the first question in the affirmative. The constitutional foundation for the Guantánamo litigation is therefore no longer in dispute. Upon taking office, the Obama Administration reaffirmed that the Guantánamo detainees have a constitutional right to challenge the lawfulness of their detention.[31] As important for present purposes was the Court's answer to the second question. The Court held that the review process created by the DTA was *not* an adequate substitute for habeas because it failed to provide the detainee with a meaningful opportunity to challenge his detention, which includes the right to challenge the allegations against him and to gather and present evidence in his favor.[32] It also failed to permit meaningful judicial review of "both the cause for detention and [of] the Executive's power to detain," and did not permit the judiciary to order release.[33]

Notably, the Court left it to the "expertise and competence of the District Court to address in the first instance" how habeas hearings should be conducted.[34] In addition, as in *Hamdi v. Rumsfeld*, the Court left to the lower courts the task of refining the substantive detention standard.[35] Some have criticized the Supreme Court for asking the lower courts to develop these rules. In her concurrence in *Al Bihani v. Bush*, for instance, Judge Brown of the D.C. Circuit complained about "the unprecedented task of developing rules to review the propriety of military actions during a time of war, relying on common law tools."[36] Respectfully, we believe these criticisms are misplaced. The Court in *Boumediene* emphatically *did not* direct the lower courts to "review the propriety of military actions."[37] Instead, it charged them with applying facts to law in order to determine whether a prisoner's detention was lawful. This is a quintessential judicial function. For centuries, during moments of calm as well as crisis, courts have done precisely that. Moreover, the lower courts have not been inventing law; they have been interpreting and applying a standard for detention set by President George W. Bush in 2004, in the wake of *Rasul*, and refined by President Barack Obama in 2009. Interpreting and applying standards set by Congress or the Executive is also a quintessential judicial function.

Nor is it unusual for the Supreme Court to task the lower courts with developing either the procedures or the substantive standard that will govern a class of cases. On the contrary, as the Court observed in *Textile Workers Union of America v. Lincoln Mills of Alabama*, "[i]t is not uncommon for federal courts to fashion federal law where federal rights are concerned."[38] In *Lincoln Mills*, the Court interpreted § 301 of the Labor Management Relations Act of 1947 to "authorize[ ] federal courts to fashion a body of federal law,"[39] including both the substantive law, and the "procedure for making [labor] agreements enforceable in the courts."[40] Recognizing that the unique facts presented by cases would guide the development of the law, the Court predicted confidently that "[t]he range of

judicial inventiveness will be determined by the nature of the problem."[41]

Congress has likewise recognized that courts are best suited to develop the rules that will govern litigation. The Rules Enabling Act provides that "[t]he Supreme Court shall have the power to prescribe general rules of practice and procedure and rules of evidence for cases in the United States district courts."[42] The Act reflected a "[r]ecognition by Congress of the broad rule-making power of the courts"[43] and was "intended to allocate power between the Supreme Court as rulemaker and Congress."[44] Pursuant to the Act, the Supreme Court promulgated both the Federal Rules of Procedure (in 1938) and the Federal Rules of Evidence (in 1975).[45] While it is true that Congress did not accept all the rules of evidence proposed by the Supreme Court Advisory Committee,[46] and has occasionally added specific requirements to address perceived needs,[47] the overwhelming majority of the rules come initially from the Court's rulemaking power.

This is as it should be. Courts are well suited to promulgate the rules for judicial proceedings because judges know best the business of the courts. Judges are in the trenches, dealing with day-to-day needs and demands of litigants. They experience firsthand the way procedure serves the substantive law. Because of this institutional experience, they are well positioned to develop new rules in unusual circumstances, and to adjust those rules as experience demands. Former Attorney General Homer Cummings, at whose behest the bill for the Rules Enabling Act was introduced, remarked on the desirability of having the courts issue rules:

> Legislative bodies have neither the time to inquire objectively into the details of judicial procedure nor the opportunity to determine the necessity for amendment or change. Frequently such legislation has been enacted for the purpose of meeting particular problems or

supposed difficulties, but the results have usually been confusing or otherwise unsatisfactory.[48]

In sum, the Court in *Boumediene* fully expected habeas would work, and directed the lower courts to make it so. In the sections that follow, we discuss the resulting jurisprudence in some detail. Before digging in, however, it is useful to take a closer look at two cases that have been decided by the District Court. These cases serve as exemplars and frame the discussion that follows. They reveal the complexity of the issues presented by the Guantánamo litigation, as well as the subtlety of the courts' substantive and procedural rules.

III. A Tale of Two Cases

We set forth below the details of two habeas cases as described in the opinions. In one case, the judge granted the habeas petition; in the other it was denied.

A. *Al Rabiah*[49]

In December, 2001, Fouad Al Rabiah, a Kuwaiti, was seized by Afghan villagers near Jalalabad as he attempted to flee unarmed into Pakistan.[50] The villagers turned him over to American authorities, who brought him to Guantánamo in May 2002. Al Rabiah insisted he was innocent, and that he had traveled to Afghanistan to complete a fact-finding mission regarding Afghanistan's refugee problem and medical infrastructure.[51] The government, however, said his purpose was more sinister. According to the government, he was "not an aspiring aid worker caught up in the front lines of the United States war against al-Qaeda" but rather a "devotee of Osama bin Laden who ran to bin Laden's side after September 11th."[52] In the government's favor, several witnesses identified him as a member of al Qaeda and associate of Bin Laden who fought in the Tora Bora mountains.[53] And when the government confronted Al Rabiah at Guantánamo with these accusations, he repeatedly confessed, sometimes in great detail.[54]

Yet, as set forth in the court's opinion, the government's case had problems. There was the matter of Al Rabiah's personal background. At the time of his capture, he was 43 years old and the father of four.[55] For twenty years he had worked at Kuwait Airways, where his supervisor said he had a "spotless attendance record" and "was never absent without leave."[56] He had no military training, "except for two weeks of compulsory basic training with the Kuwait Army, after which he was medically discharged

due to a knee injury."[57] When taken into custody by the Americans, he was overweight at 240 pounds, and suffered from high blood pressure and chronic neck and back pain.[58]

He also had a long history of traveling "to impoverished and/or war-torn countries for charitable purposes."[59] In 1994, he traveled to Bosnia to volunteer for the Revival of Islamic Heritage Society.[60] In 1998, he went to Kosovo, where he volunteered for the Kuwait Red Crescent.[61] In 2000, he was part of a mission to Bangladesh with the Patients Helping Fund, where he delivered kidney dialysis fluid to a facility in Dakka.[62] In July 2001, he traveled to Afghanistan for ten days, and in October 2001, he went back to Afghanistan, intending to stay for approximately two weeks.[63] Al Rabiah said the trips to Afghanistan were merely a continuation of the charitable work he had done for years.[64] Prior to his fateful trip to Afghanistan in October 2001, he took the precaution of requesting two weeks' leave from his position at Kuwait Airlines, and while he was in Afghanistan wrote letters to his family describing his aid work.[65]

The court found that the witnesses against Al Rabiah did not provide convincing evidence against him. By the time of Al Rabiah's hearing, the government had withdrawn reliance on almost everything these witnesses had said. One witness alleged Al Rabiah "was in charge of supplies at Tora Bora."[66] But according to the court, this witness's allegations were "filled with inconsistencies and implausibilities," which included a collection of inconsistent allegations against other prisoners.[67] Another witness said Al Rabiah gave bin Laden money, served "in various fighting capacities" at Tora Bora, and provided money to the *mujahideen* in Bosnia in 1995.[68] But "the only consistency" about this witness's allegations, the court observed, "is that they repeatedly change[d] over time."[69] Some allegations were "demonstrably false" and others were simply unreliable.[70] The witness had, for instance, misidentified individuals about whom he had given information.[71] The allegation of the final witness was not based on first hand information, was uncorroborated by other evidence, and had been made only after he had been subjected to a week of sleep deprivation; this witness did not repeat the allegation either before or after the sleep deprivation program.[72]

By the time of the hearing, the government had withdrawn its reliance on most of the allegations leveled by these witnesses.[73] But Al Rabiah's interrogators believed them at the time they were made, and as the court pointed out, "sought to have Al Rabiah confess to them."[74] In addition, they told Al Rabiah that unless he confessed, he would stay at Guantánamo forever.[75] As a result, all his confessions "follow the same pattern":

> Interrogators first explain to Al Rabiah the "evidence" they have in their possession . . . . Al Rabiah then requests time to pray (or to think more about the evidence) before making a "full" confession. Finally, after a period of time, Al Rabiah provides a full confession to the evidence through elaborate and incredible explanations that the interrogators themselves do not believe. This pattern began with his confession that he met with Usama bin Laden, continued with his confession that he undertook a leadership role in Tora Bora, and repeated itself multiple other times with respect to "evidence" that the Government has not even attempted to rely on as reliable or credible.[76]

By this process, interrogators produced a collection of confessions they eventually came to believe were untrue.[77] "Even beyond the countless inconsistencies," the court noted, the confessions were "entirely incredible."[78] According to the government, Al Rabiah, "a 43 year old who was overweight, suffered from health problems, and had no known history of terrorist activities or links to terrorist activities," traveled to Afghanistan, where he had never been prior to 2001, "and began telling senior al Qaeda leaders how they should organize their supplies in a six square mile mountain complex that he had never previously seen and that was occupied by people whom he had never previously met, while at the same time acting as a supply logistician and mediator of supply disputes that arose among various fighting factions."[79] All this from a man who "had no military experience except for two weeks of compulsory basic training in Kuwait, after which he received a medical exemption."[80]

In the final analysis, the court observed that "[t]he Government's simple explanation for the evidence in this case is that Al Rabiah made confessions that the court should accept as true. The simple response is that the Court does not accept confessions that even the Government's own interrogators did not believe. The writ of habeas corpus shall issue."[81] The government did not appeal.

B. *Al Odah*[82]

Contrast *Al Rabiah* with *Al Odah*. Fawzi Al Odah was born in Kuwait City, Kuwait, in 1977, and received his degree in Islamic studies from Kuwait University in 1998.[83] Prior to 2001, he often traveled to Saudi Arabia for family vacations or to visit holy sites, and traveled to Pakistan in 2000 to teach along the border between Pakistan and Afghanistan.[84] On August 13, 2001, he left for Afghanistan.[85] Al Odah said he made the trip because he believed the Afghan people "would be very receptive to his teachings."[86] He took three weeks leave from work, and planned to spend two weeks in Afghanistan.[87]

Al Odah's account of his travels had certain inconsistencies. He traveled to Afghanistan, for instance, via Dubai, and said he remained in Dubai for about a week.[88] In fact, however, he stayed there only overnight.[89] Al Odah eventually traveled to Spin Buldak, an Afghan town near the Pakistan border, where he went to a mosque and promptly asked "to meet someone affiliated with the Taliban," ostensibly "to assist him in traveling to places to teach."[90] He later said he taught in Spin Buldak approximately two weeks, but could not "describe any details associated with his teaching activities."[91] On September 10, 2001, at the direction of the Taliban official he had met, he traveled to Kandahar.[92] But not only did this extend his trip beyond the two weeks originally planned, it meant his route of travel—Dubai, Karachi, Quetta, Spin Buldak, and Kandahar—was the same as that followed by a number of people who entered Afghanistan for purposes of jihad.[93]

In the Kandahar area, Al Odah attended a Taliban camp where he took one day of training on an AK-47.[94] He was still in the Kandahar area on September 11.[95] At the hearing, Al Odah claimed that after September 11, he "only wanted to leave Afghanistan."[96] Yet this was inconsistent both with his testimony at a prior administrative proceeding at Guantánamo and with his actual behavior.[97] Instead of making the 124 mile trip south from Kandahar to Quetta, Pakistan, Al Odah traveled *away* from the border toward Kabul, 350 miles to the north.[98] This pattern repeated itself until Al Odah's capture in December 2001 after the battle in Tora Bora. Repeatedly he had the opportunity to leave the country by a direct route; repeatedly he eschewed that opportunity and traveled closer to the area of conflict, following the same route as that of al Qaeda and Taliban fighters.[99] Even after he separated from his initial Taliban contact, "Al Odah continued to take directions from individuals who were associated with the Taliban and continued to meet and travel with individuals who appeared to be fighters . . . . He made these choices while, at the same time, also choosing to surrender his passport, accept a weapon, and travel with a large group of armed men into the Tora Bora mountains."[100] And he still had this weapon—an AK-47— when he was captured.[101] "Taken as a whole, the Court f[ound] that this record makes it more likely than not that Al Odah became part of the Taliban's forces."[102]

* * * *

The different results in these two cases cannot be attributed to different judicial philosophies, as both were decided by the same judge. And while we take no position on either outcome, it is abundantly clear the court's decisions were reached only after a thorough adversarial presentation, followed by a careful parsing of the entire record and a discerning assessment of witness credibility. More than anything, the two cases demonstrate the capacity of the judiciary to resolve these cases in a prudent, cautious, and discriminating manner. Today, Al Rabiah is home with his family, and Al Odah is in U.S. custody.

IV. Federal Courts' Standard for Who May Be Detained at Guantánamo

In *Hamdi v. Rumsfeld*,[103] the Supreme Court held that the authorization in the AUMF to use "'necessary and appropriate force' includes the power to detain combatants subject to such force" when captured on the battlefield.[104] The Court clarified that the "authority to detain for the duration of [a] relevant conflict . . . is based on long-standing law-of-war principles,"[105] but left to the lower courts the task of developing the substantive standard that would govern habeas proceedings.[106] The Court delegated this responsibility in recognition of the judiciary's "time-honored and constitutionally mandated roles of reviewing and resolving claims like those presented [by *habeas* petitioners]."[107] In *Boumediene v. Bush*, the Court reaffirmed its faith in the lower courts and left to them the important job of refining the substantive standard.[108] Complying with the Court's directive, the lower courts are steadily progressing toward a workable detention standard. In the process, they have produced a body of law that provides a predictive framework for litigants and useful guidance for the government and intelligence agencies in the current military campaigns.[109] So long as it acts within constitutional limits, Congress is certainly empowered to step in. But there is no indication that such action is necessary. A careful study of the jurisprudence post-*Boumediene* shows that attacks on the judiciary's role are unfounded.

A. *Boumediene*

The first District Court case to address the substantive detention standard was *Boumediene v. Bush* on remand from the Supreme Court.[110] Judge Leon declined the litigants' invitation to "draft" a detention standard, and

chose instead to look for a standard that had been put forward by the political branches and that comported with the AUMF and Article II.[111] The court asserted that its role, upon locating such a definition, was merely to "interpret the meaning of the definition as it applies to the facts in any given case."[112]

With that role in mind, the court adopted the detention standard used by the Department of Defense in Combatant Status Review Tribunals (CSRTs), concluding that it had been both drafted by the Executive and endorsed by Congress:

> An "enemy combatant" is an individual who was part of or supporting Taliban or al Qaeda forces, or associated forces that are engaged in hostilities against the United States or its coalition partners. This includes any person who has committed a belligerent act or has directly supported hostilities in aid of enemy armed forces.[113]

When the court applied this standard to the merits of the case, it found that five of the six petitioners in *Boumediene* could not be detained, but that the sixth was lawfully detained because the government had shown he had helped others travel to take up arms against the United States.[114] The court reasoned that "facilitating the travel of others to join the fight against the United States in Afghanistan constitutes direct support to al-Qaida in furtherance of its objectives and that this amounts to 'support' within the meaning of the 'enemy combatant' definition."[115]

Judge Leon subsequently clarified this detention standard by applying it in other habeas cases pending before him. In one case he found the government met its burden by presenting evidence that a detainee stayed at al Qaeda and Taliban guest houses where he surrendered his passport, trained at a Taliban camp, traveled to two fronts to support fighting forces, and remained with a Taliban unit until well after September 11, 2001.[116] In another case, he upheld the detention of a detainee who "stayed at an al Qaeda affiliated guesthouse in Afghanistan, . . . received military training at an al Qaeda affiliated training camp, and . . . supported the Taliban in its fight against the Northern Alliance and U.S. forces as a member of the 55th Arab Brigade" by serving as a cook for the Taliban's fighting forces, carrying a weapon, and taking orders from Taliban military personnel.[117] In yet another case, Judge Leon found that a petitioner's detention was not justified, holding that the government had failed to sustain its burden when it relied almost entirely on two Guantánamo detainees whose "credibility and reliability . . . ha[d] either been directly called into question by Government personnel or has been characterized by Government personnel as undetermined."[118]

B. *Gherebi*

The Obama Administration adopted a detention standard similar but not identical to that of the Bush Administration:

> The President has the authority to detain persons that the President determines planned, authorized, committed, or aided the terrorist attacks that occurred on September 11, 2001, and persons who harbored those responsible for those attacks. The President also has the authority to detain persons who were part of, or substantially supported, Taliban or al Qaida forces or associated forces that are engaged in hostilities against the United States or its coalition partners, including any person who has committed a belligerent act, or has directly supported hostilities, in aid of such enemy armed forces.[119]

The first sentence of this standard "is taken almost verbatim from the AUMF."[120] As to the second, the Obama Administration maintained that detention requires "substantial" support for the Taliban, al Qaeda, or associated forces.[121] But as with decisions reached during the Bush Administration, courts have not been called upon to draft a detention standard. Rather, they have been asked to interpret and apply a standard provided to them by the political branches.

Two judges have offered extended interpretations of the Obama Administration's proposed standard. In *Gherebi v. Obama*, Judge Walton examined the scope of the Executive's authority to "detain individuals as part of its ongoing military campaign against [al Qaeda and the Taliban]."[122] Judge Walton adopted the following standard:

> [T]he President has the authority to detain persons who were part of, or substantially supported, the Taliban or al-Qaeda forces that are engaged in hostilities against the United States or its coalition partners, provided that the terms "substantially supported" and "part of" are interpreted to encompass only individuals who were members of the enemy organization's armed forces, as that term is intended under the laws of war, at the time of their capture.[123]

This language largely tracks the Obama Administration's proposal. The only qualification by the court was to interpret the key terms—"substantially supported" and "part of"—to require evidence the petitioner was a "member [ ] of the enemy organization's armed forces," within the meaning of the law of war.[124]

Expanding on the "membership" requirement, Judge Walton held that the government could "detain anyone who is a member of the 'armed forces' of an organization that '[the Executive] determines planned, authorized, committed, or aided' the 9/11 attacks, as well as any member of the 'armed forces' of an organization harboring the members of such an organization."[125] An "organization," as Judge Walton understood it, meant a group "organized . . . under a command responsible . . . for the conduct of its subordinates."[126] The court found "there is a distinction to be made between members of a terrorist organization involved in combat operations and civilians who may have some tangential connections to such organizations."[127] A member need not be a fighter, but he must belong to the organization's command structure. "[M]ere sympathy for or association with an enemy organization does not render an individual a member of that enemy organization's armed forces. Instead, the individual must have some sort of 'structured' role in the 'hierarchy' of the enemy force."[128]

Based on this understanding, the court held that the government's powers do not reach "[s]ympathizers, propagandists, and financiers" who are outside the command structure.[129] "At the same time, the armed forces of the enemy consist of more than those individuals who would qualify as 'combatants' in an international armed conflict. The key question is whether an individual 'receive[s] and execute[s] orders' from the enemy force's combat apparatus, not whether he is an al-Qaeda fighter."[130] Under this standard,

> an al-Qaeda member tasked with housing, feeding, or transporting al-Qaeda fighters could be detained as part of the enemy armed forces notwithstanding his lack of involvement in the actual fighting itself, but an al-Qaeda doctor or cleric, or the father of an al-Qaeda fighter who shelters his son out of familial loyalty, could not be detained assuming such individuals had no independent role in al-Qaeda's chain of command.[131]

Consistent with the common law tradition, and recognizing that he could not anticipate all questions that future cases might present, Judge Walton declined to determine "the precise nature and degree of 'substantial support,' or the precise characteristics of 'associated forces,' that are or would be sufficient to bring persons and organizations within the government's proposed standard for detention."[132] Instead, he left the standard for future courts to refine on a case-by-case basis.[133]

C. *Hamlily*

In *Hamlily v. Obama*,[134] Judge Bates further refined and clarified the scope of the government's detention authority. Where Judge Walton in *Gherebi* insisted on "membership," Judge Bates said the petitioner must be "part of" a group hostile to the United States, as such language is understood by the law of war.

> [T]he Court concludes that under the AUMF the President has the authority to detain persons that the President determines planned, authorized, committed, or aided the terrorist attacks that occurred on September 11, 2001, and persons who harbored those responsible for those attacks. The President also has the authority to detain persons who are or were part of Taliban or al Qaeda forces or associated forces that are engaged in hostilities against the United States or its coalition partners, including any person who has committed (*i.e.*, directly participated in) a belligerent act in aid of such enemy armed forces.[135]

Thus, like Judge Walton in *Gherebi*, Judge Bates held that the government's detention authority extended to individuals who directly participated in belligerent acts, or who "planned, authorized, committed, or aided the terrorist attacks that occurred on September 11, 2001," as well as individuals who are or were "part of" the Taliban or al Qaeda.[136] Despite the different formulations, however, Judge Bates noted that in application, the difference between *Gherebi* and *Hamlily* "should not be great."[137] Evidence tending to demonstrate that a petitioner provided substantial support, as required by Judge Walton's understanding of membership, would also tend to establish the detainee was "part of" a covered organization or "committed a belligerent act" through direct participation in hostilities.[138]

Like Judge Walton, Judge Bates recognized the importance of having a specific set of facts to consider when shaping the contours of the law, and declined to specify the criteria for being "part of" an organization, leaving the question to case-by-case development.[139] He did, however, note that the approach would be "more functional than formal."[140] Under this standard, a court would consider not just a petitioner's self-identification, but "whether the individual functions or participates within or under the command structure of the organization"[141]— again similar to the standard in *Gherebi*.

A number of judges have applied *Hamlily*. In *Al Ginco v. Obama*, Judge Leon cited *Hamlily* when holding that an individual who was imprisoned by al Qaeda and the Taliban and was tortured into confessing he was a U.S. spy was not "part of" those organizations.[142] Similarly, Judge Kollar-Kotelly adopted the *Hamlily* standard in *Al Mutairi v. United States*, holding that traveling without a passport on the same routes as al Qaeda and the Taliban, coupled with the appearance of the detainee's name on a published list of purported captured al Qaeda fighters, where evidence suggested that the list was made by a prison guard to alert the prisoners' families of their whereabouts, does not establish that the petitioner was "part of" the enemy's organization.[143] And in *Awad v. Obama*, Judge Robertson applied *Hamlily* in holding that evidence the petitioner went to Kandahar to fight and was in Mirwais Hospital when al Qaeda forces resisted a siege from U.S. and affiliated forces was enough to establish the petitioner was "part of" al Qaeda, though Judge Robertson believed the evidence was "gossamer thin."[144]

In sum, there has emerged a consensus view at the District Court about the basic contours of the detention standard. The standards articulated in *Hamlily* and *Gherebi* are functionally the same. Both standards provide that the government bears the burden of proving by a preponderance of the evidence that a petitioner committed a belligerent act or was a member of (or "part of") an enemy organization's armed forces. Both standards use a functional analysis to determine membership, which the *Gherebi* court read into the "substantial support" prong of the government's proposed standard, and the *Hamlily* court read into the "part of" prong. Thus, under both

standards, the courts consider circumstantial evidence of membership, not just a petitioner's self-identification. Critical to this analysis is whether a petitioner was part of the command and control structure of an enemy organization. What this reveals is the gradual exploration and shaping of the detention standard by the courts, based on the AUMF and the law of war and guided by factual considerations presented by the cases before them. This is a role well suited to the courts because it draws on the core competencies of the judiciary.

D. *Al-Bihani*

The D.C. Circuit recently addressed the government's detention authority. In *Al-Bihani v. Obama*,[145] the court considered the appeal of a detainee whose petition had been denied by Judge Leon, who had applied the standard proposed by the Bush Administration.[146] Under this standard, the government may detain anyone "who was part of or supporting Taliban or al Qaeda forces, or associated forces that are engaged in hostilities against the United States or its coalition partners."[147] The D.C. Circuit held that the law of war was irrelevant to the Executive's detention power, and that the appropriate standard was that which had been employed by the Bush Administration rather than the refinement offered by the Obama Administration.[148] The court held that Al-Bihani could be detained regardless of whether the support he provided to the Taliban was "substantial."[149] Although this standard may yet be further refined by continuing litigation, there is no reason to doubt the ability of the three-level federal court system to develop a substantive detention standard. For Congress to legislate an entirely new detention standard would be to fix what is not broken.

V. District Court Procedures for Resolving Individual Cases

Since *Boumediene*, the federal courts have moved prudently and incrementally towards a resolution of the Guantánamo cases. Shortly after the Supreme Court decision, the District Court judges asked former Chief Judge Thomas Hogan to draft a Case Management Order (CMO) to govern the litigation. Such orders, which typically set the basic rules and deadlines for litigants, are routine in civil litigation and are used by district judges to manage everything from the simplest tort cases to the most complex multi-district litigation. Judge Hogan's CMO—issued after full briefing and argument[150]— established the framework for both discovery and merits hearings. His order quickly became the model for the entire bench, which has promoted the development and application of a uniform procedural framework.[151] At the same time, however, the courts have administered the CMO with flexibility, adjusting deadlines and controlling the litigation as individual cases require—usually at the request of the government. The result is a standard, cautious, and predictable set of rules that has given rise to a rational jurisprudence. In this section, we describe the jurisprudence, and divide the discussion between discovery and merits.[152]

A. Procedures for Protecting Classified Information

The risk that classified information will be wrongfully released to the public has been a central concern throughout the Guantánamo habeas litigation. To meet this concern, and using the considerable expertise they have developed applying the Classified Information Procedures Act (CIPA), the lower courts have fashioned a set of rules that seeks to strike a careful balance between protecting classified information and ensuring that petitioners have enough information to challenge their detention. These rules fall into two categories: restrictions on counsel and restrictions on the detainee. With respect to the former, no attorney may travel to Guantánamo, meet with a detainee, or receive and review classified material unless he or she has first received a security clearance based on a thorough background investigation by the FBI. In other words, every attorney authorized to see classified information and meet with a detainee has been cleared to do so by the FBI. Even after receiving security clearances, however, counsel must agree in writing to comply with a strict Protective Order which not only lays out counsel's obligations with respect to classified information, but also warns counsel of the potential consequences, including possible criminal sanctions, should they violate the Order. One requirement of the Protective Order bars counsel from disclosing classified information to any detainee, including his or her client. Furthermore, all classified documents released by the government are stored in a secure facility in the Washington, D.C., area that is staffed by the Department of Justice 24 hours a day and closed to the public.

With respect to restrictions on the detainee, the CMO obligates the government to disclose to the petitioner the unredacted copies of documents on which it relies or that are exculpatory.[153] The government may, however, redact portions of the documents disclosed that are not exculpatory,[154] and at least one court has suggested that the burden falls on the petitioner to show that redacted portions of documents are in fact exculpatory.[155] The government may also file for an exception to the disclosure requirement. If the government invokes this provision, the court will conduct an *in camera* review of information for which the government seeks an exception to determine whether it is relevant and material.[156] Moreover, the fact that the government discloses documents to the detainee does not make those documents public; under the Protective Order, whatever the detainee shares with counsel is presumptively classified and cannot be further disclosed unless reviewed by the government and determined to be unclassified. In addition, the detainee's personal letters and even legal mail are screened by the government, which means the detainee cannot divulge classified information he learns to the outside world. In short, the District Court has taken elaborate precautions to ensure that no classified information is mishandled or inadvertently disclosed.

B. Discovery Standards

In issuing its decree, the Supreme Court in *Boumediene* recognized the District Court judges would not be writing on a blank slate. There are certain well-established evidentiary principles that govern most any adversarial proceeding. As the first step toward implementing the constitutional right recognized in *Boumediene*, the CMO entitles detainees to three categories of evidence: 1) exculpatory evidence (*i.e.*, evidence in the government's possession that materially tends to exculpate a detainee); 2) evidence that the government relies on; and 3) additional evidence if and only if the detainee can show good cause.[157]

1. The Duty to Disclose Exculpatory Evidence

The CMO directs the government to disclose "to the petitioner all reasonably available evidence in its possession that tends materially to undermine the information presented to support the government's justification for detaining the petitioner."[158] This language raises two questions: where does the government have to look (*i.e.*, what evidence is "reasonably available"?), and what does the government have to disclose (*i.e.*, what evidence "tends materially to undermine" the case for detention?). With respect to the former, the District Court judges have held that the government's obligation to uncover and disclose "reasonably available" evidence is satisfied if it searches the computer files compiled by three entities: the Joint Intelligence Group (JIG) of the Joint Task Force-Guantánamo (JTF-GTMO); the Office for the Administrative Review of the Detention of Enemy Combatants (OARDEC); and the Guantánamo Task Force established by President Obama's January 22, 2009, Executive Order.[159]

This issue seems settled and is no longer the subject of extensive litigation; petitioners who ask the government to search beyond these databases under § I.D.1 of the CMO have generally met with little success.[160] Courts also limit discovery under § I.D.1 if the petitioner's request is overly broad. Courts have refused to order the government to turn over information allegedly referenced in other cases if the reference lacks specificity, is redundant, or is not analogous to the case at hand.[161] Courts are particularly skeptical of "fishing expeditions" and have universally rejected requests that ask for "any and all" exculpatory evidence.[162]

Judges have held that evidence "tends materially to undermine" the case for detention if it "undercuts the reliability and/or credibility of the government's evidence."[163] Other judges have developed substantially similar formulations.[164] Some judges have provided additional guidance. Judge Huvelle, for example, found that "evidence that casts doubt on a speaker's credibility, evidence that undermines the reliability of a witness's identification of the petitioner, or evidence that indicates a statement is unreliable because it is the product of abuse, torture, or mental or physical incapacity" tends to materially undermine the government's case.[165] And Judge Kessler held in *Al-Adahi v. Bush* that exculpatory evidence "includes any evidence of abusive treatment, torture, mental incapacity, or physical incapacity which could affect the credibility and/or reliability of evidence being offered."[166] For many years, courts have recognized that evidence procured by torture cannot be used to justify a prisoner's detention. Under this formulation, petitioners are permitted to argue a particular statement was tainted by unreliable interrogation methods—an argument the courts are free to reject. In any event, we do not understand these various formulations to announce different or incompatible standards, nor has the government suggested otherwise. They are merely alternative articulations of the same rule.

Applying this rule, courts have found a variety of evidence to be exculpatory, including evidence that a bounty or other payment was made for the capture of the petitioner;[167] evidence that a third party witness was tortured;[168] and negative identifications by other detainees.[169] Under § I.D.1, courts usually consider evidence of abuse to be exculpatory if the abuse took place close in time to the statement that the government wishes to use against the detainee.[170] However, detainees who allege that exculpatory information regarding torture exists must make sufficiently specific requests for that information.[171] Finally, once the government has certified that it has produced all exculpatory evidence, the judges tend to give deference to that certification.[172]

2. The Duty to Disclose Evidence Relied on by the Government

The CMO also directs the government to disclose "(1) any documents and objects in the government's possession that the government relies on to justify detention; (2) all statements, in whatever form, made or adopted by the petitioner that the government relies on to justify detention; and (3) information about the circumstances in which such statements of the petitioner were made or adopted."[173]

Requests for documents and objects that the government relies upon to justify detention must be specific.[174] In making their determinations, the courts may give deference to the government's representations that it did not rely on the information requested by petitioners.[175] In *Bin Attash v. Obama*, for instance, the court accepted the government's claim that, in support of its case, it would only rely upon intelligence reports revealing that the petitioner had certain detonating devices, but would not attempt to rely upon the devices themselves. Under § I.E.1(1), therefore, the government was only required to disclose the reports, not the devices.[176] Courts sometimes require that the government produce an underlying document rather than the intelligence report that referenced it.[177] These determinations are necessarily made on a case-by-case basis and depend on the factual circumstances surrounding the evidence.

If the government relies on statements made by a petitioner, it must produce all reasonably available forms and versions of the petitioner's statements.[178] This includes "audio recordings of statements;" "video recordings of statements;" "transcripts of statements;" "contemporaneous notes taken during statements;" or "records or reports of statements prepared by persons other than the persons who prepared the summaries of the statements already produced."[179] In addition, the judges require that the government disclose "(1) the identity of the speaker; (2) the content of the statement; (3) the person(s) to whom the statement was made; (4) the date and time the statement was made or adopted; and (5) the circumstances under which such statement was made or adopted (including the location where the statement was made)," or indicate that it is unable to identify the source or context of the information it relies upon.[180] The government's burden to produce statements, like its burden with respect to exculpatory evidence, is limited to that which is reasonably available. Absent a specific showing under § I.E.2, the government is only required to search the Joint Intelligence Group (JIG) of the Joint Task Force-

Guantánamo (JTF-GTMO); the Office for the Administrative Review of the Detention of Enemy Combatants (OARDEC); and the Executive Task Force files for statements of petitioners.[181]

The CMO also obligates production of evidence regarding the circumstances surrounding statements used by the government. This information allows the courts to assess, on a case-by-case basis, whether such statements can support further detention.[182] Time, location, duration, physical conditions, coercion, promises, and copies of interrogation logs are discoverable.[183] Courts have allowed discovery for "any evidence of coercive techniques used during any interrogation or any inducements or promises made;"[184] "all reports, interviews, interrogations, and statements—including tapes, transcripts, and original notes;"[185] "interrogation plans, plan forms, logs or similar records pertaining to that statement, including records relating to efforts to 'soften up' the petitioner prior to interrogation;"[186] and negative identifications in which other detainees could not identify the petitioner as a participant in the conduct alleged by the government.[187]

3. Additional Discovery Only if the Detainee Can Show "Good Cause"

Upon request, petitioners automatically receive exculpatory evidence and the evidence relied on by the government. All other discovery is discretionary and requires that the petitioner establish good cause. Requests for additional discovery, governed by §I.E.2 of the CMO, must "(1) be narrowly tailored, not open-ended; (2) specify the discovery sought; (3) explain why the request, if granted, is likely to produce evidence that demonstrates that the petitioner's detention is unlawful; and (4) explain why the requested discovery will enable the petitioner to rebut the factual basis for his detention without unfairly disrupting or unduly burdening the government."[188] The courts have consistently and scrupulously demanded that petitioners' requests meet all four requirements before granting additional discovery.[189]

As noted earlier, requests for "any and all" documents demonstrating a particular proposition have been universally rejected as too broad. For example, in *Sadkhan v. Obama*, Judge Collyer rejected a request for "any and all" statements made by the petitioner.[190] Judge Collyer found that the petitioner's request was overly broad, was not likely to produce exculpatory evidence, and was unduly burdensome for the government.[191] Other examples of courts rejecting requests as overbroad include requests for a petitioner's or a witness's "complete file,"[192] and requests for all medical records.[193]

On the other hand, courts often grant requests that are specific and limited. Evidence that a detainee or a witness against him was tortured, the circumstances surrounding coercive interrogations, and selected medical records may be discoverable under § I.E.2 so long as the requests are narrowly tailored.[194] Information regarding the use of a translator by an interrogator may also be discovered under § I.E.2 if the request is sufficiently specific.[195] Courts sometimes allow extremely limited discovery with the expectation that more discovery may be granted in the future based on the information the government produces.[196] Using this progressive discovery method, courts seek to assess the evidentiary needs of each petitioner and the unique facts in the case without overburdening the government or jeopardizing secure information. Finally, courts will only consider requests for additional discovery that seek reasonably available evidence.[197] And even if requests are narrowly tailored, they will be rejected if they are unlikely to produce evidence helpful to the detainee.[198]

C. How Procedures Permit Cases to Be Resolved in an Orderly and Judicious Fashion

Just as the lower courts have developed a coherent and uniform jurisprudence regarding discovery, they have crafted a set of procedures that permits the orderly resolution of merits disputes.

1. The Standard of Proof

The Supreme Court in *Boumediene* did not specify the "showing required of the Government" in the Guantánamo habeas proceedings.[199] Some detainees argued that the prospect of indefinite detention obligated the government to prove its allegations beyond a reasonable doubt, akin to that required in a criminal case, or by clear and convincing evidence, akin to that employed in deportation or civil commitment cases.[200] Judge Hogan's CMO, however, requires only that the government prove the lawfulness of the petitioner's detention by a preponderance of the evidence.[201] As noted above, this was the standard proposed by the government. Judges Walton and Bates adopted this standard in *Gherebi* and *Hamlily*, other judges followed suit,[202] and it was recently endorsed by the D.C. Circuit.[203] A detainee need not prove he was acting innocently or testify on his own behalf.[204]

2. Presumptions of Authenticity and Accuracy

In *Hamdi*, the Court suggested that a rebuttable presumption "in favor of the government's evidence" might be appropriate.[205] From this, the government has often asked the judges to presume its evidence is both authentic and accurate. The two presumptions, however, are very different. A presumption of authenticity means the evidence is at least presumptively what it purports to be, which in turn relieves the government of any further obligation to lay a proper foundation for the item's admissibility; a presumption of accuracy, by contrast, means the content of the item in question—an interrogation report, for instance—is presumptively correct.

In general, the judges have been much more likely to presume authenticity than accuracy. In *Al-Adahi v. Obama* and *Ali Ahmed v. Obama*, for example, Judge Kessler granted the government's request for a presumption of

authenticity.[206] Judge Kessler relied on the "business records" hearsay exception,[207] which allows the admission of hearsay evidence for evidence kept in the course of regularly conducted business activity. Because the government represented that all of its documents were maintained in the ordinary course of business and the petitioner presented no evidence to the contrary, the court found the evidence authentic.[208]

As Judge Kessler recognized, however, a presumption of authenticity is rebuttable, and occasionally, courts have found that petitioners have successfully rebutted the presumption.[209] For example, in *Al Rabiah*, *Al Mutairi*, and *Al Odah*, the courts found significant reason to doubt that the government's evidence was what it purported to be.[210] In each case, however, the courts deferred any ruling on whether the evidence was admissible until all the evidence had been presented by both parties.[211] This allowed the court to consider the authenticity of the evidence based on the totality of the circumstances.[212]

Unlike presumptions of authenticity, the District Court bench has denied nearly all requests for a presumption of accuracy. The courts have expressed a concern that a presumption of accuracy would tip the delicate balance of interests too far in the government's favor and intrude on the role of the court. Courts have emphasized that final decisions about the reliability, accuracy, and weight of evidence—issues which are often "hotly contested"—are best left to the fact-finder.[213] As explained by Judge Kollar-Kotelly, "One of the central functions of the Court in [these cases] is to 'evaluate raw evidence' proffered by the government and to determine whether it is 'sufficiently reliable and sufficiently probative to demonstrate the truth of the asserted proposition with the requisite degree of clarity.'"[214] Rather than allow blanket presumptions about the accuracy of evidence, the judges have preferred to examine each piece of evidence, weighing the many factors that may bear on the evidence's reliability, including its consistency with other evidence, the conditions under which the evidence was created, the accuracy of any translation or transcription, the personal knowledge of the declarant, and whether the information contained in the evidence has been recanted.[215]

3. Admission of Hearsay

In *Hamdi*, the plurality acknowledged that "[h]earsay . . . may need to be accepted as the most reliable available evidence from the government."[216] The Court reaffirmed this sentiment in *Boumediene*, stating that it expected the lower courts to exercise their discretion to accommodate the government's legitimate national security interests to "the greatest extent possible."[217] Consistent with these admonitions, the CMO provides that judges "may admit and consider hearsay evidence that is material and relevant to the legality of the petitioner's detention if the movant establishes that the hearsay evidence is reliable and that the provision of non-hearsay evidence would unduly burden the movant or interfere with the government's efforts to protect national security."[218] Consistent with 28 U.S.C. § 2246, the government may, if necessary, satisfy these conditions through the use of affidavits or declarations rather than through live testimony.

Applying the CMO, the judges have generally admitted hearsay from both petitioners and the government.[219] As Judge Kollar-Kotelly explained, "allowing the use of hearsay by both parties balances the need to prevent the substantial diversion of military and intelligence resources during a time of hostilities, while at the same time providing [the petitioner] with a meaningful opportunity to contest the basis of his detention."[220] Having thus accepted hearsay in principle, the judges have focused their inquiry on case-by-case determinations about the weight such evidence should be given. Most judges make this determination after the merits hearing, in light of entire record.[221] Under this approach, the court places the burden on the party submitting the evidence to establish its probative value.[222] The rationale for such an approach

was provided by Judge Kollar-Kotelly in *Al Rabiah*: "Rather than exclude evidence from consideration *ex ante* by examining it in a vacuum, the Court concludes that the better approach is to make such determinations after considering all of the evidence in the record and hearing the parties' arguments related thereto."[223] In making determinations about hearsay, the bench has looked to a variety of case-specific factors, including inconsistency, evidence of abuse or torture at the time the statement was made, and lack of detail in the statement.[224]

At least one judge attempted to further clarify the standard for the admissibility of hearsay evidence.[225] In *Bostan v. Obama*, Judge Walton held that the government could not rely on a shortage of resources or its own mistakes as justification for the use of hearsay.[226] Relatedly, he held that the undue burden prong of the CMO relates to the burden imposed *on the government*, not on its counsel.[227] In addition, Judge Walton stressed that the government must actually establish that the use of non-hearsay evidence would be an undue burden, and that mere allegations or conclusory representations to that effect would not suffice.[228] Finally, Judge Walton stated that hearsay proffered by the government does not become admissible simply because the government has nothing else.[229] In the final analysis, however, Judge Walton recognized that his attempt to clarify the standard of admissibility of hearsay produced largely the same result as the inquiry conducted by other judges: "Whether the assessment of a piece of hearsay's evidentiary worth is made at a preliminary hearing on the admissibility of proffered evidence or at the close of merits proceedings after being provisionally admitted into the record, the bottom line is that hearsay of no evidentiary worth will not be considered when the Court makes its factual findings."[230]

In a recent decision, the D.C. Circuit clarified the approach to questions of admissibility of hearsay evidence, settling any discrepancies between Judge Walton's admissibility-focused approach and the other judges' weight-focused approach. In *Al Bihani v. Obama*, the court observed that "the question a habeas court must ask when presented with hearsay is not whether it is admissible—it is always admissible—but what probative weight to ascribe to whatever indicia of reliability it exhibits."[231] Because judges are experienced and sophisticated fact-finders, the determinations about the weight to be given to individual pieces of evidence have not proven difficult to the District Court bench. For instance, the greater the level of detail in a hearsay statement, the more likely the court is to find it reliable.[232] In *Ahmed v. Bush*, one of the four witnesses on whom the government relied could only report that he overheard statements. He could not recall any details of the conversation, nor could he relate the circumstances in which the statements were made, nor could he identify the speakers he supposedly overheard.[233] The court refused to credit the witness's statements.[234] As this decision implies, the witness's credibility is an important factor in deciding what weight to give contested hearsay.[235] Courts are far less willing to credit witnesses who have made unreliable accusations in the past.[236] Not surprisingly, courts are more likely to be persuaded by hearsay evidence if it is corroborated by other evidence.[237] Conversely, hearsay evidence that is inconsistent with other, undisputed evidence is unlikely to be persuasive to the court.[238] Finally, the courts are more likely to find a witness who consistently tells the same story credible than one who has told differing accounts, particularly when the differences may be attributable to the use of aggressive interrogation techniques.[239] In *Al Rabiah*, for instance, the court found that a witness who only made statements during sleep deprivation techniques, and not before or after, was not reliable and that his testimony should not be considered probative.[240] The following section more fully addresses the courts' rulings on the use of involuntary statements.

4. Totality of the Circumstances Test for Involuntary Statements

In many cases, the petitioner has argued that statements used by the government were obtained as a result of abuse or torture. Neither the Supreme Court nor the D.C. Circuit has spoken directly to how such evidence should be treated by the District Court. However, the District Court judges have developed a consistent jurisprudence in an attempt to decide when courts should admit allegedly involuntary statements, how much weight those statements should be given, and whether previous abuse taints subsequent statements.

The court's approach to determining the weight of involuntary statements grows logically out of its approach to hearsay. Using all the evidence offered by both parties, the judges have employed an individualized test that looks to the totality of the circumstances to determine the weight to be given to allegedly involuntary statements.[241] A case-by-case determination allows the court to consider all the factors surrounding each allegedly involuntary statement to determine the reliability and accuracy of the proffered statement, seeking to maintain a balance between the interests of the government and the petitioner.[242] In *Bacha v. Obama*, for instance, Judge Huvelle suppressed all statements made by the petitioner after finding that they had been secured by torture.[243] In the same way, Judge Hogan in *Anam v. Obama* found that 23 of the 26 statements by the petitioner, Musa'ab Omar Al Madhwani, offered by the government lacked "sufficient indicia of reliability" because they were obtained through the application of "harsh interrogation techniques."[244] In short, where the totality of circumstances suggests that allegations of abuse are credible and that coerced statements are unreliable, the courts will not admit the statements, or will accord them no weight. By contrast, however, the courts have also made clear that mere allegations of torture are not sufficient. In *Awad v. Obama*, the petitioner claimed his statements had been coerced.

Although the discussion of the alleged coercion is relatively short and largely redacted, it appears that Judge Robertson found that the "only specific allegation of coercion is the claim that interrogators threatened to withhold medical treatment."[245] But this allegation was belied by the interrogators' notes, which indicated that Awad had received medical care.[246] Judge Robertson therefore rejected the allegation.

In several cases, the government has conceded that abuse occurred but argued that subsequent statements should nonetheless be admitted. Courts resolve this issue by applying a test borrowed from the criminal law, asking whether there was a "clean break" between the coercion and the subsequent statement.[247] The government bears the burden of showing that the prior coercion did not taint the later statement.[248] In *Anam*, for example, Judge Hogan found no "clean break" between the petitioner's abusive detention in Afghanistan and twenty-three of his subsequent statements to interrogators at Guantánamo Bay.[249] The evidence suggested that interrogators at Guantánamo "relied on, or had access to, Petitioner's coerced confessions from Afghanistan," indicating a connection between the prior and subsequent statements.[250] Likewise, in *Al Rabiah*, Judge Kollar-Kotelly refused to credit statements by the petitioner when the government failed to provide evidence to suggest that the taint from previous abuse had dissipated by the time the petitioner made the disputed statements.[251]

5. Case-by-Case Inquiry to Determine Whether a Relationship between a Petitioner and a Terrorist Group Has Been Vitiated

In some cases, petitioners have argued that, although they once had relationships with al Qaeda or the Taliban, they were not "part of" the organizations at the time of their capture. These arguments have led the courts to consider "whether a prior relationship between a detainee and al Qaeda (or the Taliban) can be sufficiently vitiated by the passage of time, intervening events, or both, such

that the detainee could no longer be considered to be 'part of' either organization at the time he was taken into custody."[252]

There is a strong consensus that detention is lawful if the government can prove that *at the time of capture* the petitioner was part of or substantially supporting al Qaeda or the Taliban. Using this as a general standard, Judges Leon, Kessler, Urbina and Bates have all ruled that the government may not lawfully detain a petitioner whose relationship with al Qaeda or the Taliban ended prior to the petitioner's capture.[253] In *Al Ginco*, Judge Leon granted the writ after finding that the petitioner's relationship with al Qaeda ended before he was taken into custody. In that case, the government effectively conceded that Janko had been imprisoned and tortured by al Qaeda and the Taliban when the organizations accused him of being a U.S. spy.[254] To analyze whether the relationship between the petitioner and the organizations had ended, Judge Leon examined three factors: "(1) the nature of the relationship in the first instance; (2) the nature of the intervening events or conduct; and (3) the amount of time that has passed between the time of the pre-existing relationship and the point in time at which the detainee is taken into custody."[255] Applying these factors, the court found that the brief pre-existing relationship between Janko and al Qaeda was "total[ly] eviscerated" by the torture and imprisonment at the hands of al Qaeda.[256]

Other judges have conducted similar analyses to grant the writ to detainees whose relationships with al Qaeda and the Taliban were vitiated prior to the petitioners' capture. In *Hatim*, Judge Urbina found that the government failed to disprove the petitioner's argument that he'd removed himself from the command structure of al Qaeda prior to his capture.[257] Citing to *Al Ginco*, Judge Kessler concluded in *Al Adahi* that the petitioner's short relationship with al Qaeda was vitiated when he was expelled from a training camp for failing to follow orders and had cut off ties to al Qaeda following his expulsion.[258]

Addressing a related issue, Judge Huvelle has found that a petitioner's relationship with a terrorist organization may be effectively vitiated *after* capture.[259] In *Basardh v. Obama*, Judge Huvelle held that the government may lawfully detain only those individuals who remain a security threat to the United States, even if the individual was "part of" a terrorist organization at the time of his capture. In *Basardh*, the court found that "the undisputed facts establish that Basardh's [redacted] is known to the world, and thus, any ties with the enemy have been severed, and any realistic risk that he could rejoin the enemy has been foreclosed."[260] In other words, the petitioner's post-capture conduct sufficiently vitiated the relationship with al Qaeda. Thus far, Judge Huvelle is the only judge to have made such a finding, and her approach has been explicitly rejected by at least one other District Court judge.[261]

6. Courts' Rejection of the "Mosaic Theory" as a Means for the Government to Meet Its Burden

In some cases, the government has urged the judges to apply a "mosaic theory" to its evidence.[262] Originally used as a strategy for intelligence analysis, the mosaic theory maintains that pieces of evidence should be evaluated as a whole, rather than assessed independently.[263] Judge Leon was the first to address the theory directly.[264] In *El Gharani v. Obama*, the government claimed its evidence consisted of a "mosaic of allegations," including statements by the petitioner and fellow detainees as well as certain classified documents. Judge Leon, however, found that the "mosaic theory" could not make up for deficiencies in the evidence. He acknowledged the "substantial and troubling uncertainties regarding [the] petitioner's conduct" but found that, ultimately, the government failed to carry its burden.[265] "[A] mosaic of tiles bearing images this murky reveals nothing about the petitioner with sufficient clarity, either individually or collectively, that can be relied upon by this Court."[266] Judge Kessler has voiced a similar concern.[267] The mosaic theory, she said, "is only

as persuasive as the tiles which compose it and the glue which binds them together."[268]

Judges Leon and Kessler agree the mosaic theory cannot magically transform unreliable evidence into its opposite. While other judges have not addressed the mosaic theory explicitly, the structure of their analysis suggests that a consistent jurisprudence is developing with respect to the mosaic theory. In determining whether detention is lawful, the District Court bench examines the reliability and credibility of each allegation or statement relied on by the government. Though the government need not prove the accuracy of every piece of evidence it presents, when it fails to prove *any* allegations, the mosaic theory cannot shore up the deficiencies. The courts have found that any other rule would effectively lower the burden of proof in a way that would tip the scales too far in favor of the government and undermine *Boumediene's* promise to maintain the essential safeguards of the Great Writ.

D. Release Orders

In fashioning relief in cases decided in favor of the detainee, courts have ordered the government "to take all necessary and appropriate diplomatic steps to facilitate [the petitioner's] release forthwith."[269] Most judges do not set a specific time by which the petitioner must be released nor do they specify the measures the government must take. In *Kiyemba v. Obama*, the court ordered the release into the United States of 17 Chinese Uighurs who, by the government's admission, posed no threat to the United States.[270] The D.C. Circuit reversed, holding that the authority to exclude an alien was exclusively held by the political branches and could not be superseded by the courts.[271] The Supreme Court granted *certiorari*,[272] and while the case was pending, many of the petitioners had been resettled and all had received offers of resettlement.[273] On March 1, 2010, the Supreme Court vacated the decision of the D.C. Circuit and remanded the case to determine the impact of these new factual developments.[274] On May 28, 2010, the D.C. Circuit reinstated its earlier opinion.[275]

VI. Responding to the Criticism

It is evident to us that the federal courts are developing a coherent and consistent jurisprudence that attempts to balance the liberty interests of the prisoner against the security interests of the United States. As we have noted, however, some observers have suggested otherwise. The Brookings Institution, for example, released a report arguing that the federal judges are serving as "default legislators" who are drafting "the substantive law of detention itself."[276] But the courts are doing no such thing. Instead, they are doing what courts in this country are uniquely qualified to do and what they do every day—*namely*, interpreting and applying a substantive standard that has been given to them by the political branches. That standard, as indicated above, is as follows:

> The President has the authority to detain persons that the President determines planned, authorized, committed, or aided the terrorist attacks that occurred on September 11, 2001, and persons who harbored those responsible for those attacks. The President also has the authority to detain persons who were part of, or substantially supported, Taliban or al Qaida forces or associated forces that are engaged in hostilities against the United States or its coalition partners, including any person who has committed a belligerent act, or has directly supported hostilities, in aid of such enemy armed forces.[277]

As noted earlier, the courts have applied this standard in a collection of cases. There is no need to repeat that discussion here. Suffice it to say, however, that the very serious and disturbing charge leveled by individuals at Brookings that federal courts are engaged in improper "lawmaking" is wholly unfounded.

The Brookings report also complains that the courts have reached inconsistent results, and calls for a legislative solution. This has been echoed by some political figures. Senator Lindsey Graham (R-SC), for instance, said Congress needs to "change our laws [and] come up with better guidance" for judges.[278] As we have stressed throughout this report, Congress is certainly empowered, within constitutional limits, to draft new legislation. But as we have attempted to demonstrate, close examination of the jurisprudence reveals that what some critics describe as inconsistent applications is, rather, the *consistent application of the same standard to different fact patterns*. Unsurprisingly, this sometimes leads to different results, but that is a virtue of the common law process, not a fault, for it means that judges are providing precisely the individualized review required by the law and demanded by justice. That different judges may offer modestly different articulations of the same standard is equally unremarkable.

In this regard, it bears noting that the Department of Justice, which represents the United States in this litigation, understands that the wide range of factual scenarios presented by these cases can only be resolved by the common law process. When the Obama Administration drafted the detention standard quoted above, it provided the following interpretive guidance to the courts:

> There are cases where application of the terms of the AUMF and analogous principles from the law of war will be straightforward. *It is neither possible nor advisable, however, to attempt to identify, in the abstract, the precise nature and degree of "substantial support," or the precise characteristics of "associated forces," that are or would be sufficient to [justify a person's detention]* . . . . [T]he particular facts and circumstances justifying detention will vary from case to case, and may require the identification and analysis of various ana-

logues from traditional international armed conflicts. Accordingly, the contours of the "substantial support" and "associated forces" bases of detention will need to be further developed in their application to concrete facts in individual cases.[279]

Indeed, even if Congress were to draft a code, that too would be subject to judicial interpretation. Even the most detailed regulatory schemes require litigation to define the meaning of terms in specific cases. Congressional involvement at this stage, therefore, would not clarify the law. On the contrary, it would throw the jurisprudence into disarray and require years of additional litigation just to return to the point we have now reached post-*Boumediene*.

VII. Conclusion

The Guantánamo litigation has tested the judiciary as it has tested the nation. But the judiciary, like the country and the Constitution it serves, has risen to the challenge. As former judges, we do not doubt for an instant that Congress has the power, within constitutional limits, to draft a detailed code that would set this litigation on yet a new direction. Congress could, within limits, write a new detention standard for the courts to apply. Congress could, within limits, write different procedural rules to govern this litigation. But such a course is at once unwise and unnecessary: unwise because it would bring us back to square one just when the courts are finally beginning to resolve these cases; and unnecessary because the federal bench, as it has done for centuries, is steadily developing a coherent and rational jurisprudence. Habeas is working.

VIII. Appendix: Table of Habeas Cases

Table of Habeas Cases Resolved by the United States District Court for the District of Columbia

Case	Judge	Decision	Appeal status
Abdah v. Obama (Petitioner's name: Uthman)	Kennedy	Habeas granted	None filed yet
Abdah v. Obama (Petitioner's name: Odaini)	Kennedy	Habeas granted	None filed yet
Ahmed v. Obama	Kessler	Habeas granted	None – Petitioner transferred
Al Adahi v. Obama	Kessler	Habeas granted	Appealed
Al Ginco v. Obama	Leon	Habeas granted	None – Petitioner transferred
Al Harbi (Petitioner's name: Ravil Mingazov)	Kennedy	Habeas granted	None filed yet
Al Mutairi v. U.S.	Kollar-Kotelly	Habeas granted	None – Petitioner transferred
Al Rabiah v. U.S.	Kollar-Kotelly	Habeas granted	None – Petitioner transferred
Bacha v. Obama (Petitioner's name: Jawad)	Huvelle	Habeas granted	None – Petitioner transferred
Basardh v. Obama	Huvelle	Habeas granted	Appealed
Boumediene v. Bush (Petitioners' names: Boudella, Boumediene, Idir, Lahmar, and Nechla)	Leon	Habeas granted	None – Petitioner transferred

El Gharani v. Bush	Leon	Habeas granted	None – Petitioner transferred
Hatim v. Obama	Urbina	Habeas granted	Appealed
Mohammed v. Obama	Kessler	Habeas granted	Appealed
Slahi v. Obama	Robertson	Habeas granted	Appealed
Uighur cases[1]	Urbina	Habeas granted	Some appealed, some petitioners transferred
Abdah v. Obama (Petitioner's name: Esmail)	Kennedy	Habeas denied	None filed yet
Al Adahi v. Obama (Petitioner's name: al Nahdi)	Kessler	Habeas denied	Appealed
Al Adahi v. Obama (Petitioner's name: al Assani)	Kessler	Habeas denied	Appealed
Al Alwi v. Bush	Leon	Habeas denied	Appealed
Al Bihani v. Obama	Leon	Habeas denied	Appealed – Affirmed
Al Odah v. U.S.	Kollar-Kotelly	Habeas denied	Appealed
Al Warafi v. Obama	Lamberth	Habeas denied	Appealed
Anam v. Obama (Petitioner's name: Al Madhwani)	Hogan	Habeas denied	Appealed
Awad v. Obama	Robertson	Habeas denied	Appealed
Barhoumi v. Obama	Collyer	Habeas denied	Appealed

[1] The decision to grant habeas to 17 Uighur petitioners was made by District Court Judge Urbina on October 7, 2008. *See In re Guantánamo Bay Detainee Litigation*, 581 F. Supp. 2d 33 (D.D.C. 008).

Boumediene v. Bush (Petitioner's name: Bensayah)	Leon	Habeas denied	Appealed
Hammamy v. Obama	Leon	Habeas denied	Appealed
Khalifh v. Obama	Robertson	Habeas denied	None filed yet
Sliti v. Bush	Leon	Habeas denied	Appealed

IX. Endnotes

[1] 128 S. Ct. 2229 (2008).

[2] Brief on Behalf of Former Federal Judges as Amici Curiae in Support of Petitioners, *Boumediene v. Bush*, 128 S. Ct. 2229 (2008) (Nos. 06-1195, 06-1196), 2007 WL 2441585.

[3] *Hamdi v. Rumsfeld*, 542 U.S. 507, 535 (2004) (O'Connor, J., plurality opinion).

[4] 583 F. Supp. 2d 133 (D.D.C. 2008).

[5] 609 F. Supp. 2d 43 (D.D.C. 2009).

[6] *Id.* at 53 & n.4, 67.

[7] *Id.* at 71.

[8] 616 F. Supp. 2d 63 (D.D.C. 2009).

[9] *Id.* at 69.

[10] *Id.* at 76.

[11] *Anam v. Obama*, 653 F. Supp. 2d 62, 64 (D.D.C. 2009).

[12] 590 F.3d 866 (D.C. Cir. 2010).

[13] *In re Guantánamo Bay Detainee Litigation*, No. 08-mc-0442, 2008 WL 4858241 (D.D.C. Nov. 6, 2008), *amended by* 2008 WL 5245890, § I.D.1 (D.D.C. Dec. 16, 2008) [hereinafter CMO] (case management order).

[14] *Al-Adahi v. Bush*, 585 F. Supp. 2d 78, 79–80 (D.D.C. 2008).

[15] CMO, *supra* note 13, § I.E.1 (citation omitted).

[16] *Id.* § I.E.2.

[17] *In re Guantánamo Bay Detainee Litigation*, 581 F. Supp. 2d 33, 43 (D.D.C. 2008), *rev'd sub nom. Kiyemba v. Obama*, 555 F.3d 1022 (D.C. Cir. 2009).

[18] 128 S. Ct. 2229 (2008).

[19] *See Al Bihani v. Obama*, 590 F.3d 866, 881–86 (D.C. Cir. 2010) (Brown, J., concurring) (expressing concern about the judiciary's ability to develop the rules to review military actions); Benjamin Wittes et al., *The Emerging Law of Detention: The Guantánamo Cases as Lawmaking* (Governance Studies at Brookings, 2010; U. of Texas Law, Public Law Research Paper No. 165, 2010), *available at* http://ssrn.com/abstract=1540601 (characterizing the courts as fundamentally disagreeing on the substantive and procedural standards for habeas cases brought by Guantánamo detainees); Chisun Lee, *Judges Urge Congress to Act on Indefinite Terrorism Detentions*, Pro Publica, Jan. 22, 2010, http://www.propublica.org/feature/judges-urge-congress-to-act-on-indefinite-terrorism-detentions-122 (describing three trial judges' concerns about the judiciary making policy decisions with respect to the law of detention without guidance from Congress).

[20] *Rasul v. Bush*, 542 U.S. 507 (2004).

[21] *See Al Odah v. United States*, 321 F.3d 1134 (D.C. Cir. 2003).

[22] 339 U.S. 763 (1950).

[23] *See Al Odah*, 321 F.3d at 1141 ("We cannot see why, or how, the writ [of habeas corpus] may be made available to aliens abroad when basic constitutional protections are not."); *Rasul v. Bush*, 215 F. Supp. 2d 55, 68 (D.D.C. 2002) (holding that "aliens detained outside the sovereign territory of the United States [may not] invok[e] a petition for a writ of habeas corpus").

24 *Rasul*, 542 U.S. at 470.

25 *Id.* at 476.

26 *Id.* at 481–82 (footnotes omitted).

27 DTA § (e)1005, 119 Stat. 2742.

28 548 U.S. 557, 576–84 (2006).

29 28 U.S.C. § 2241(e) (Supp. 2007).

30 *Boumediene v. Bush*, 128 S. Ct. 2229, 2241–42 (2008). This process included a Combatant Status Review Tribunal (CSRT) followed by limited review in the D.C. Circuit. *Id.* at 2241.

31 Review and Disposition of Individuals Detained at the Guantánamo Bay Naval Base and Closure of Detention Facilities, Exec. Order No. 13,492, 74 Fed. Reg. 4,897 (Jan. 27, 2009).

32 *Boumediene*, 128 S. Ct. at 2270 ("Federal habeas petitioners long have had the means to supplement the record on review, even in the postconviction habeas setting. Here that opportunity is constitutionally required." (citations omitted)). The Court explained that this right relates to the reviewing court's "authority to admit and consider relevant exculpatory evidence that was not introduced during the earlier proceeding." *Id.*

33 *Id.* at 2266, 2269.

34 *Id.* at 2276.

35 542 U.S. 507, 522 n.1 (2004) (O'Connor, J., plurality opinion) ("The permissible bounds of the [enemy combatant] category will be defined by the lower courts as subsequent cases are presented to them.").

36 *Al Bihani v. Obama*, 590 F.3d 866, 881 (D.C. Cir. 2010) (Brown, J., concurring); *see also, e.g.*, Wittes et al., *supra* note 19, at 3, 81.

37 *Id.*

38 353 U.S. 448, 457 (1957) (citations omitted).

39 *Id.* at 451.

40 *Id.* at 453.

41 *Id.* at 457 (citation omitted).

42 28 U.S.C. § 2072(a) (2006).

43 28 U.S.C. § 2071 Revision Notes and Legislative Reports ("Recognition by Congress of the broad rule-making power of the courts will make it possible for the courts to prescribe complete and uniform modes of procedure . . . .").

44 Stephen B. Burbank, *The Rules Enabling Act of 1934*, 130 U. Pa. L. Rev. 1015, 1025–26 (1982) (providing an in-depth and authoritative review of the history of the Rules Enabling Act).

45 The Court also promulgated rules governing bankruptcy, criminal, and appellate procedure in federal courts under the Act. *See* James C. Duff, The Federal Rules of Practice and Procedure. Administrative Office of the U.S. Courts, The Rulemaking Process: A Summary for the Bench and Bar (2007), *available at* http://www.uscourts.gov/rules/proceduresum.htm.

46 *See, e.g.*, Jack B. Weinstein & Margaret A. Berger, Weinstein's Evidence Manual § 18.01 (8th ed. 2007) (Supreme Court standards for privilege). Notably, some of the proposed rules rejected by Congress continue to be cited by courts and have become black letter law. *Id.*

47 *See, e.g.*, The United States Private Securities Litigation Reform Act of 1995, Pub. L. 104-67, 109 Stat. 737 (codified as amended in scattered sections of 15 U.S.C.) (providing special procedural rules for matters under the federal security laws).

48 28 U.S.C. § 2071 Revision Notes and Legislative Reports (2006) (quoting Homer Cummings, *The New Criminal Rules—Another Triumph of the Democratic Process*, 31 A.B.A. J. 236, 237 (1945)).

49 *Al Rabiah v. United States*, 658 F. Supp. 2d 11 (D.D.C. 2009).

50 *Id.* at 41.

51 *Id.* at 21 (citations omitted).

[52] *Id.* (internal quotation marks and citations omitted).

[53] *Id.* at 24–27.

[54] *Id.* at 30.

[55] *Id.* at 20.

[56] *Id.* (citations omitted).

[57] *Id.* (citation omitted).

[58] *Id.*

[59] *Id.*

[60] *Id.*

[61] *Id.*

[62] *Id.*

[63] *Id.* at 20, 23.

[64] *Id.* at 21.

[65] *Id.* at 23.

[66] *Id.* at 24 (citation omitted).

[67] *Id.* at 24–25.

[68] *Id.* at 25.

[69] *Id.*

[70] *Id.* at 26.

[71] *Id.*

[72] *Id.* at 27.

[73] *Id.* at 28.

[74] *Id.*

[75] *Id.* at 39.

[76] *Id.* at 30.

[77] *Id.* at 34.

[78] *Id.*

[79] *Id.*

[80] *Id.*

[81] *Id.* at 42.

[82] *Al Odah v. United States*, 648 F. Supp. 2d 1 (D.D.C. 2009), *appeal pending*, No. 09-5331 (D.C. Cir.).

[83] *Id.* at 8.

[84] *Id.*

[85] *Id.*

[86] *Id.* (citation and internal quotation marks omitted).

[87] *Id.*

[88] *Id.*

[89] *Id.*

[90] *Id.* at 9 (citation and internal quotation marks omitted).

[91] *Id.*

[92] *Id.*

[93] *Id.*

[94] *Id.* at 10. Though not essential to the decision, the court found this camp was more likely than not Al Farouq, the primary al Qaeda training facility in Afghanistan. *Id.* at 8. The court held, however, that Al Odah's detention was lawful whether the camp was run by the Taliban or al Qaeda. *Id.* at 18.

[95] *Id.* at 11.

[96] *Id.*

[97] *Id.* at 11–12.

[98] *Id.* at 12.

[99] *Id.* at 13 & n.15

[100] *Id.* at 14–15.

[101] *Id.* at 15.

[102] *Id.*

[103] 542 U.S. 507 (2004) (O'Connor, J., plurality opinion).

[104] *Al-Bihani v. Obama*, 590 F.3d 866, 872 (D.C. Cir. 2010) (quoting *Hamdi*, 542 U.S. at 519).

[105] *Hamdi*, 542 U.S. at 521.

[106] *Id.* at 522 n.1 ("The legal category of enemy combatant has not been elaborated upon in great detail. The permissible bounds of the category will be defined by the lower courts as subsequent cases are presented to them.").

[107] *Id.* at 535 (citation omitted).

[108] 128 S. Ct. 2229, 2276 (2008) ("These and the other remaining questions are within the expertise and competence of the District Court to address in the first instance").

[109] That the courts have proven themselves up to this task should come as no surprise; for centuries, and throughout this country's history, the challenge of deciding whether a prisoner's detention is lawful has fallen to the judiciary. *See, e.g.*, WILLIAM F. DUKER, A CONSTITUTIONAL HISTORY OF HABEAS CORPUS (1980); *see also* Paul D. Halliday & G. Edward White, *The Suspension Clause: English Text, Imperial Contexts, and American Implications*, 94 VA. L. REV. 575, 591 n.35 (2008) (noting at least 143 documented habeas cases in England during the three centuries before 1789).

[110] 583 F. Supp. 2d 133, 134 (D.D.C. 2008) (mem.).

[111] *Id.*

[112] *Id.*

[113] *Id.* at 135 (congressional approval was demonstrated by the inclusion in the definition of "unlawful enemy combatants" those individuals who had been deemed such by CSRTs).

[114] *Boumediene v. Bush*, 579 F. Supp. 2d 191, 197–98 (D.D.C. 2008).

[115] *Id.* at 198.

[116] *Al Alwi v. Bush*, 593 F. Supp. 2d 24, 27–28 (D.D.C. 2008). Surrendering passports is a common Al Qaeda practice. *Id.* at 28.

[117] *Al Bihani v. Obama*, 594 F. Supp. 2d 35, 38–40 (D.D.C. 2009), *aff'd* 590 F.3d 866, 872 (D.C. Cir. 2010).

[118] *El Gharani v. Bush*, 593 F. Supp. 2d 144, 147 (D.D.C. 2009).

[119] *See, e.g.*, *Hamlily v. Obama*, 616 F. Supp. 2d 63, 67 (D.D.C. 2009) (footnote omitted).

[120] *Id.* at 67 n.5.

121 *Gherebi v. Obama*, 609 F. Supp. 2d 43, 53 (D.D.C. 2009).

122 *Id.* at 45.

123 *Id.* at 71.

124 *Id.*

125 *Id.* at 67 (quoting Authorization for Use of Military Force (AUMF), Pub. L. No. 107-40, § 2(a), 115 Stat. 224, 224 (2001)).

126 *Id.* at 68 (quoting Protocol Additional to the Geneva Conventions of 12 August 1949, and relating to the Protection of Victims of International Armed Conflicts, art. 43.1, adopted June 8, 1977, 1125 U.N.T.S. 3 (alteration in original)).

127 *Id.*

128 *Id.*

129 *Id.* at 68–69.

130 *Id.* at 68–69 (alterations in original) (citations omitted).

131 *Id.* at 69 & n.19 (citing J.K. Kleffner, *From "Belligerents" to "Fighters" and Civilians Directly Participating in Hostilities—the Principle of Distinction in Non-International Armed Conflicts One Hundred Years after the Second Hague Peace Conference*, 54 NETHERLANDS INT'L L. REV. 315, 334 (2007) ("[P]ersons who accompany the armed forces without actually being members thereof should be immune from being made the object of attack, unless and for such time as they directly participate in hostilities.")).

132 *Id.* at 69 (citation omitted).

133 *Id.* ("Certainly, there is no shortage of scenarios arising out of the conflict at hand from which to identify these contours."). As Judge Walton anticipated, other judges have adopted and refined his standard. *See, e.g., Ali Ahmed v. Obama*, 613 F. Supp. 2d 51 (D.D.C. 2009); *Al-Adahi v. Obama*, No. 05-cv-280, 2009 WL 2584685 (D.D.C. Aug. 21, 2009).

134 616 F. Supp. 2d 63 (D.D.C. 2009).

135 *Id.* at 77–78.

136 *Id.*

137 *Id.* at 76.

138 *Id.* at 76–77. The court explained, "For example, if the evidence demonstrates that an individual did not identify himself as a member, but undertook certain tasks within the command structure or rendered frequent substantive assistance to al Qaeda, whether operational, financial or otherwise, then a court might conclude that he was a 'part of' the organization. Of course, such determinations are highly fact-intensive and will be made on an individualized, case-by-case basis, applying the conclusions reflected in this decision." *Id.*

139 *Id.* at 77.

140 *Id.* at 75.

141 *Id.*

142 626 F. Supp. 2d 123, 127–31 & n.7 (D.D.C. 2009).

143 644 F. Supp. 2d 78, 85, 96 (D.D.C. 2009).

144 646 F. Supp. 2d 20, 27 (D.D.C. 2009).

145 *Al Bihani v. Obama*, 590 F.3d 866 (D.C. Cir. 2010).

146 *Id.* at 870 & n.1.

147 *Id.* at 872 (quoting *Al Bihani v. Obama*, 594 F. Supp. 2d 35, 38, 40 (D.D.C. 2009)). On appeal, the Obama Administration advanced its revised standard, which required not mere "support," but "substantial support." *See id.* at 870 n.1.

148 *Id.* at 871–72.

149 *Id.* at 872.

[150] Judge Hogan issued the CMO in November 2008. *In re Guantánamo Bay Detainee Litigation*, No. 08-mc-0442, 2008 WL 4858241 (D.D.C. Nov. 6, 2008) (case management order). After considering several objections lodged by the government, Judge Hogan modified the CMO to accommodate the government's representations regarding the hardships it said his prior order would produce. *See* Government's Motion for Clarification and Reconsideration of This Court's November 6, 2008 Case Management Order and Supplemental Amended Orders or, in the Alternative, Motion For Certification for Appeal Pursuant to 28 U.S.C. § 1292(B) and To Stay Certain Obligations Pending Resolution of The Motion and Any Appeal, *In re Guantánamo Bay Detainee Litigation*, No. 08-mc-442 (D.D.C. Nov. 18, 2008). The Amended CMO, which remains in place, extended the time for the government to file a factual return, limited the government's obligation to produce evidence, and clarified the government's duties with respect to the production of exculpatory evidence, the procedures for dealing with classified information, and the petitioner's duty to file a traverse. *See* CMO, *supra* note 13.

[151] *See infra* Section I.V.C.

[152] As we have repeatedly stressed, the authors take no position on the substantive decisions issued by the lower courts. It is inevitable that some of us would have decided at least some of these issues differently. That is a normal and salutary aspect of the common law process. Rather, our point is that the jurisprudence—taken as a whole—has developed in a rational, judicious fashion, precisely as contemplated by the Supreme Court, and that attacks on the judiciary are therefore misplaced.

[153] *Bin Attash v. Obama*, 628 F. Supp. 2d 24, 36 (D.D.C. 2009) (discovery order); *Al-Adahi v. Obama*, 597 F. Supp. 2d 38, 42 (D.D.C. 2009) (discovery order).

[154] *Darbi v. Obama*, No. 05-cv-2371, 2009 WL 5511160, at *5-6 (D.D.C. Dec. 22, 2009) (discovery order).

[155] *Id.*

[156] *Al Odah v. United States*, 559 F.3d 539, 543 (D.C. Cir. 2009); *Bin Attash*, 628 F. Supp. 2d at 36 (discovery order).

[157] CMO, *supra* note 13, §§ I.D.1, I.E.1, I.E.2.

[158] *Id.* § I.D.1.

[159] *Al-Adahi v. Obama*, 597 F. Supp. 2d 38, 41 n.3 (D.D.C. 2009) (discovery order); *Bin Attash*, 628 F. Supp. 2d at 38 ("[I]n accordance with other judges of this Court, the Court will consider that information compiled by the Executive Task Force created by President Obama's January 22, 2009 Executive Order is reasonably available information." (footnote omitted)); *Zaid v. Obama*, 616 F. Supp. 2d 119, 121 n.2 (D.D.C. 2009) (discovery order) (in discussing § I.D.1, the court wrote: "The Court previously interpreted the 'automatic discovery' provisions of the CMO (i.e., discovery available under § I.E.1) to require searches of only the 'consolidated assemblages of information' created by the Joint Intelligence Group ('JIG') of the Joint Task Force-Guantánamo ('JTF-GTMO') and the Office for the Administrative Review of the Detention of Enemy Combatants ('OARDEC')."); *Razak v. Obama*, No. 05-cv-1601, 2009 WL 1322603, at *1 (D.D.C. May 11, 2009) (discovery order); *Al Ansi v. Obama*, No. 08-cv-1923, 2009 WL 1287981, at *1 (D.D.C. May 11, 2009) (discovery order); *Alhami v. Obama*, No. 05-cv-359, 2009 WL 1286861, at *1 (D.D.C. May 11, 2009) (discovery order) ("reasonably available evidence" under § I.D.1 includes "any evidence discovered during the ongoing review of Guantánamo cases ordered by President Obama on January 22, 2009" (citation omitted)); *Ameziane v. Obama*, No. 05-cv-392, 2009 WL 1158843, at *1 (D.D.C. Apr. 30, 2009) (discovery order); *Al-Oshan et al. v. Obama*, No. 05-cv-0520 , slip op. at 3 (D.D.C. Apr. 23, 2009) (discovery order); *Abdah v. Obama*, No. 04-cv-1254, slip op. at 5 (D.D.C. Apr. 8, 2009) (discovery order).

[160] We know of only one order in which the court has required the government to search beyond the consolidated file under § I.D.1. *See Zaid*, 616 F. Supp. 2d at 121.

[161] *See Rabbani v. Obama*, 608 F. Supp. 2d 62, 67 (D.D.C. 2009) (discovery order).

[162] *See, e.g., Sadkhan v. Obama*, 608 F. Supp. 2d 33, 38 (D.D.C. 2009) (discovery order) (rejecting a request for "any and all" statements made by the petitioner).

[163] *See, e.g., Ameziane v. Obama*, No. 05-cv-392, 2009 WL 691124, at *1 (D.D.C. Mar. 6, 2009) (discovery order); *Zemiri v. Bush*, No. 04-cv-2046, 2009 WL 311858, at *1 (D.D.C. Feb. 9, 2009) (discovery order); *Al-Mithali v. Bush*, No. 05-cv-2186, 2009 WL 71517, at *1 (D.D.C. Jan. 9, 2009) (discovery order); *Abdessalam v. Bush*, No. 06-cv-1761, slip op. at 2 (D.D.C. Dec. 19, 2008) (discovery order).

[164] *See, e.g., Al Odah v. United States*, No. 02-cv-828, 2009 WL 382098, at *1 (D.D.C. Feb. 12, 2009) (discovery order).

[165] *See, e.g., Amenziane*, 2009 WL 691124, at *1; *Al-Mithali*, 2009 WL 71517, at *1; *Abdessalam*, No. 06-cv-1761, slip op. at 2.

[166] *See, e.g., Al-Adahi v. Bush*, 585 F. Supp. 2d 78, 79–80 (D.D.C. 2008) (case management order).

[167] *Bin Sa'Adoun Alsa'ary v. Obama*, 631 F. Supp. 2d 9, 16 (D.D.C. 2009); *Rabbani v. Obama*, 608 F. Supp. 2d 62, 67–68 (D.D.C. 2009) (discovery order).

[168] *Bin Attash v. Obama*, 628 F. Supp. 2d 24, 40 (D.D.C. 2009) (discovery order) (ordering the disclosure of physically or psychologically coercive measures used against third parties and including medical records).

[169] *Al Ansi v. Obama*, 647 F. Supp. 2d 1, 7 (D.D.C. 2009) (discovery order).

[170] *Bin Attash*, 628 F. Supp. 2d at 39 (ordering the Government to turn over all reasonably available evidence of abuse during the time the petitioner was in custody.); *id.* (evidence of torture that occurred prior to or simultaneous to petitioners statements is exculpatory); *see also Lnu v. Obama*, 656 F. Supp. 2d 187, 194 (D.D.C. 2009) (discovery order) ("[E]xculpatory evidence" includes reasonably available evidence of "abusive treatment, torture, or mental or physical incapacity prior to or contemporaneous with the time that petitioner gave any statements that are included in the factual return.").

[171] *Compare Al-Adahi v. Obama*, 607 F. Supp. 2d 131, 133 (D.D.C. 2009) (denying petitioner's request for evidence of torture because the government certified that it had produced all exculpatory evidence and because petitioner did not allege specific instances of torture), *with Lnu*, 656 F. Supp. 2d at 193–94 (finding that the petitioner's allegations are sufficiently specific under § I.D.1 and ordering the government to produce all reasonably available evidence of torture).

[172] *See Rabbani*, 608 F. Supp. 2d at 65 ("Because the respondents have already stated that they have provided the evidence required under § I.D.1 [for reasonably available evidence]. . . . . . . [T]he court analyzes the petitioner's request under § I.E.2.").

[173] CMO, *supra* note 13, § I.E.1 (citation omitted). As with the disclosure of exculpatory evidence, the courts have restricted discovery of evidence on which the government relies to include only that which is reasonably available to the government. *Amenziane v. Obama*, No. 05-cv-392, 2009 WL 1158843, at *1 (D.D.C. Apr. 30, 2009) (discovery order) ("This definition of 'reasonably available evidence' applies to both the government's exculpatory evidence and automatic discovery obligations.").

[174] *Bin Attash*, 628 F. Supp. 2d at 35; *Abdessalam v. Bush*, No. 06-cv-1761, slip op. at 1 (D.D.C. Dec. 19, 2008).

[175] *Bin Attash*, 628 F. Supp. 2d at 37.

[176] *Id.*

[177] *See, e.g., Razak v. Obama*, No. 05-cv-1601, 2009 WL 2222988, at *1–2 (D.D.C. July 22, 2009).

[178] *Al Wady v. Obama*, No. 08-cv-1237, 2009 WL 5031342, *6 (D.D.C. Nov. 20, 2009); *Rabbani v. Obama*, 656 F. Supp. 2d 45 (D.D.C. 2009) (the government must disclose "*all* forms of the statements made or adopted by the petitioner that the government relies on to justify detention" including any audio or video recordings, transcripts, translations, and contemporaneous notes or records); *Anam v. Obama*, No. 04-cv-1194, 2009 WL 1322637, at *1 (D.D.C. May 11, 2009) (same); *Ghanem v. Obama*, 598 F. Supp. 2d 41, 43 (D.D.C. 2009) (the government must produce all reasonably available forms of the statements on which the government relies); *Hatim v. Obama*, No. 05-cv-1429, slip op. at 2–3 (D.D.C. Feb. 17, 2009) (mem.); *see also Bin Attash*, 628 F. Supp. 2d at 37 ("As written, section I.E.1(2) requires that if respondents rely on one of petitioner's statements to justify detention, then they must produce all forms of that statement."); *Zaid v. Bush*, 596 F. Supp. 2d 11, 14 (D.D.C. 2009) (the government may not produce only the versions of petitioners' statements as they appear in the factual return).

[179] *Alhami v. Obama*, No. 05-cv-359, 2009 WL 1286861, at *1 (D.D.C. May 11, 2009) (discovery order); *Al Ansi v. Obama*, No. 08-cv-1923, 2009 WL 1287981, at *1 (D.D.C. May 11, 2009) (discovery order); *Razak v. Obama*, No. 05-cv-1601, 2009 WL 1322603, at *1 (D.D.C. May 11, 2009) (discovery order); *Halmandy v. Obama*, 612 F. Supp. 2d 45, 47 (D.D.C. 2009); *Ameziane v. Obama*, No. 05-cv-392, 2009 WL 691124, at *1 (D.D.C. Mar. 6, 2009); *accord Ali Qattaa v. Obama*, No. 08-cv-1233, 2009 WL 691130, at *1 (D.D.C. Mar. 13, 2009).

[180] *Halmandy*, 612 F. Supp. 2d at 47; *Alhami*, 2009 WL 1286861, at *1; *Al Ansi*, 2009 WL 1287981, at *1; *Abdessalam v. Bush*, No. 06-cv-1761, slip op. at 1–2 (D.D.C. Dec. 19, 2008) (discovery order); *Razak*, 2009 WL 1322603, at *1; *Ali Qattaa*, 2009 WL 691130, at *1; *Ameziane*, 2009 WL 691124, at * 1.

[181] *Al-Ghizzawi v. Obama*, 600 F. Supp. 2d 5, 6 (D.D.C. 2009) (discovery order); *Zaid*, 596 F. Supp. 2d at 14–15.

[182] CMO, *supra* note 13, § I.E.1(3).

[183] *Abdah v. Obama*, No. 04-cv-1254, slip op. at 7 (D.D.C. Apr. 8, 2009) (ordering the government to disclose "information about the time, duration, and physical conditions of the interrogation, any physically or psychologically coercive techniques used before or during the interrogation, any inducements or promises made before or during the interrogation, and copies of any interrogation logs"); *see also Rabbani*, 656 F. Supp. 2d at 49–50 (quoting *Abdah*, *supra*).

[184] *Anam*, 2009 WL 1322637, at *1 (citing *Zaid v. Bush*, No. 05-cv-1646 (D.D.C. Dec. 22, 2008)).

[185] *Al Ansi v. Obama*, 647 F. Supp. 2d 1, 7 (D.D.C. 2009) (discovery order).

[186] *Rabbani*, 656 F. Supp. 2d at 50.

[187] *Al Ansi*, 647 F. Supp. 2d 7.

[188] CMO, *supra* note 13, § I.E.2.

[189] *See, e.g., Zaid v. Obama*, No. 05-cv-1646, 2009 WL 2136790, at *1–2 (D.D.C. June 19, 2009) (discovery order) (granting a narrow request for documents sufficient to identify a translator present at an interrogation); *Sadkhan v. Obama*, 608 F. Supp. 2d 33, 37–38, 40–41 (D.D.C. 2009) (discovery order) (denying petitioner's request under § I.E.2 for any and all statements by petitioner, any and all video recordings of the petition's statements, information surrounding the circumstances of the petitioner's statements, and the petitioner's medical records as overly broad and for failing to show that the requests would be likely to produce relevant evidence).

[190] *Sadkhan*, 608 F. Supp. 2d at 38.

[191] *Id.*

[192] *Al-Ghizzawi v. Obama*, 600 F. Supp. 2d 5, 8 (D.D.C. 2009) (discovery order) (order denying the petitioner's request for a third-party accuser's complete file, but granting the request with respect to information in the file that bears upon the accuser's credibility and/or reliability); *Al Wady v. Obama*, No. 08-cv-1237, 2009 WL 5031342, at *4 (D.D.C. Nov. 20, 2009) (order denying a request for a third-party's file because it was not specific and narrowly tailored and it had not shown that the request was likely to produce exculpatory evidence).

[193] *Lnu v. Obama*, 656 F. Supp. 2d 187, 194 (D.D.C. 2009) (discovery order) (order finding that the petitioner had failed to show that the disclosure of his medical records would be likely to undermine his detention).

[194] *Compare Abdallah v. Bush*, No. 08-cv-1923, 2009 WL 2020774, at *1 (D.D.C. July 9, 2009) (discovery order) (order granting the petitioner's request for certain medical records because, although the search for that information may have been somewhat burdensome to the government, the request was narrowly tailored enough to minimize that burden and the petitioner had shown that the evidence was likely to undermine the government's case), *with Al Ansi v. Obama*, 647 F. Supp. 2d 1, 8 (D.D.C. 2009) (discovery order) (rejecting as too broad and narrowing a request for "all medical records," and "all records of or memoranda concerning the torture or use of harsh interrogation tactics on" and "all documents concerning the credibility" of witnesses).

[195] *Zaid v. Obama*, No. 05-cv-1646, 2009 WL 2136790, at *1 (D.D.C. July 19, 2009) (discovery order).

[196] *Sadkhan v. Obama*, 608 F. Supp. 2d 33, 37 (D.D.C. 2009) (discovery order) (order rejecting a request for any and all statements of the petitioner, but ordering that the rank and agency of the government officials who reviewed the petitioner's file be disclosed to determine whether more discovery is warranted); *Al-Adahi v. Obama*, 608 F. Supp. 2d 1, 3 (D.D.C. 2009) (discovery order) (order granting in part a request for the petitioner's medical records, with the understanding that the petitioner may later "justify a particular concern" from the initial limited disclosure (records for Petitioner's first four months at GTMO) to merit further discovery).

[197] *Lnu v. Obama*, 656 F. Supp. 2d 187, 191 (D.D.C. 2009) (discovery order); *Bin Sa'Adoun Alsa'ary v. Obama*, 631 F. Supp. 2d 9, 13 (D.D.C. 2009) (discovery order).

[198] *Lnu*, 656 F. Supp. 2d at 192 (order finding that petitioner's request for information regarding other individuals associated with guest houses was narrowly tailored, but unlikely to produce exculpatory evidence and was therefore rejected); *Al Ansi*, 647 F. Supp. 2d at 7 (rejecting a request for information on release plans for other detainees because it did not demonstrate that the government's detention of the petitioner was unlawful and was unduly burdensome for the Government under § I.E.2(4)).

[199] *See Boumediene v. Bush*, 128 S. Ct. 2229, 2271 (2008) ("The extent of the showing required of the Government in these cases is a matter to be determined.").

[200] *See, e.g., Al Bihani v. Obama*, 590 F.3d 866, 878 (D.C. Cir. 2010).

201 *See* CMO, *supra* note 13, § II.A ("The government bears the burden of proving by a preponderance of the evidence that the petitioner's detention is lawful.").

202 *Al Rabiah v. United States*, 658 F. Supp. 2d 11, 25 (D.D.C. 2009); *Al-Adahi v. Obama*, No. 05-cv-280, 2009 WL 2584685, at *5 (D.D.C. Aug. 21, 2009); *Al Mutairi v. United States*, 644 F. Supp. 2d 78, 86 (D.D.C. 2009).

203 *Al Bihani*, 590 F.3d at 877.

204 *See Al Odah v. United States*, 648 F. Supp. 2d 1, 7 (D.D.C. 2009); *Ahmed v. Obama*, 613 F. Supp. 2d 51, 56 (D.D.C. 2009).

205 *Hamdi v. Rumsfeld*, 542 U.S. 507, 534 (2004).

206 *Al Adahi*, 2009 WL 2584685, at *3; *Ahmed*, 613 F. Supp. 2d at 54–55.

207 Fed. R. Evid. 803(6).

208 *See Al Adahi*, 2009 WL 2584685, at *3; *Ahmed*, 613 F. Supp. 2d at 54–55.

209 *See Al Rabiah v. United States*, 658 F. Supp. 2d 11, 17–18 (D.D.C. 2009); *Al Odah*, 648 F. Supp. 2d at 5–6; *Al Mutairi v. United States*, 644 F. Supp. 2d 78, 83–84 (D.D.C. 2009).

210 *See Al Rabiah*, 658 F. Supp. 2d at 17–18; *Al Odah*, 648 F. Supp. 2d at 5–6; *Al Mutairi*, 644 F. Supp. 2d at 83–84.

211 *See, e.g., Awad v. Obama*, 646 F. Supp. 2d 20, 23 (D.D.C. 2009).

212 In some cases, judges do not clearly distinguish between presumptions of authenticity and presumptions of accuracy. *See, e.g., Al Rabiah*, 658 F. Supp. 2d at 17–18 (discussing both presumptions in the same analysis). Judges who take this approach, such as Judge Kollar-Kotelly, typically deny the government's motion for both presumptions. *See id.*

213 *Al Adahi*, 2009 WL 2584685, at *4 ("[T]he Court must . . . make the final judgment as to the reliability of these documents, the weight to be given to them, and their accuracy.").

214 *Al Rabiah*, 658 F. Supp. 2d at 17 (citing *Parhat v. Gates*, 532 F.3d 834, 847 (D.C. Cir. 2008)).

215 *Id.*; *see also Anam v. Obama*, No. 04-cv-1194, 2010 WL 58965, at *3 (D.D.C. Jan. 6, 2010) ("The Court indicated it would determine 'the accuracy, reliability, and weight, if any, of each piece of evidence after considering the evidence as a whole and the arguments presented during the Merits Hearing . . . .'").

216 *Hamdi v. Rumsfeld*, 542 U.S. 507, 533–34 (2004).

217 *Boumediene v. Bush*, 128 S. Ct. 2229, 2276 (2008).

218 CMO, *supra* note 3, § II.C.

219 *See, e.g., Al Odah v. United States*, 648 F. Supp. 2d 1, 4–5 (D.D.C. 2009).

220 *Id.*

221 *See, e.g., Anam v. Obama*, No. 04-cv-1194, 2010 WL 58965, at *3 (D.D.C. Jan. 6, 2010); *Al Rabiah v. United States*, 658 F. Supp. 2d 11, 17 (D.D.C. 2009) ("The Court is fully capable of considering whether a piece of evidence (whether hearsay or not) is reliable, and it shall make such determinations in the context of the evidence and arguments presented during the Merits Hearing—including any arguments the parties have made concerning the unreliability of hearsay evidence." (citation omitted)).

222 *Anam*, 2010 WL 58965, at *3.

223 *Al Rabiah*, 658 F. Supp. 2d at 18.

224 *See, e.g., id.*

225 *See, e.g., Bostan v. Obama*, 662 F. Supp. 2d 1, 4 (D.D.C. 2009).

226 *Id.*

227 *Id.* at 5.

228 *Id.*

[229] *Id.*

[230] *Id.* at 7.

[231] *Al Bihani v. Obama*, 590 F.3d 866, 879 (D.C. Cir. 2010).

[232] *See, e.g., Ahmed v. Obama*, 613 F. Supp. 2d 51, 57 (D.D.C. 2009); *Boumediene v. Bush*, 579 F. Supp. 2d 191, 196 (D.D.C. 2008); *cf. Parhat v. Gates*, 532 F.3d 834, 846–47 (D.C. Cir. 2008). In *Parhat*, the D.C. Circuit found that the lack of corroborating information on reported activities recorded in intelligence documents prevented the court from assessing the reliability of the assertions in the documents. *Id.* As a result, the court found that the assertions could not sustain the determination that the appellant was an enemy combatant. *Id.* at 847. *Parhat*, however, was a review under the Detainee Treatment Act of a determination by a Combatant Status Review Tribunal, rather than the appeal of a *de novo* habeas proceeding in the district court.

[233] *Ahmed*, 613 F. Supp. 2d at 57.

[234] *Id.*

[235] *See id.* (finding the unreliability of the witness a factor in refusing to credit his testimony).

[236] *Id.*

[237] *Al Rabiah v. United States*, 658 F. Supp. 2d 11, 21 (D.D.C. 2009); *see also Boumediene v. Bush*, 579 F. Supp. 2d 191, 197 (D.D.C. 2008) ("To support its claim . . . the Government relies exclusively on the information contained in a classified document from an unnamed source. This source is the only evidence in the record directly supporting each detainee's alleged knowledge of, or commitment to, this supposed plan. And while the Government has provided some information about the source's credibility and reliability, it has not provided the Court with enough information to adequately evaluate the credibility and reliability of this source's information." (citing *Parhat*, 532 F.3d at 847)).

[238] *Al Rabiah*, 658 F. Supp. 2d at 25 (witness claimed Al Rabiah was in Afghanistan at a feast with Osama Bin Laden when it was undisputed he was out of the country).

[239] *Id.*

[240] *Id.* at 27.

[241] *See Anam v. Obama*, No. 04-cv-1194, 2010 WL 58965, at *4 (D.D.C. Jan. 6, 2010); *Mohammed v. Obama*, No. 05-cv-1347, 2009 WL 4884194, at *23 (D.D.C. Dec. 16, 2009); *Al Rabiah*, 658 F. Supp. 2d at 36, 40. The use of a case-by-case, totality of circumstances approach is hardly surprising; the courts have used a totality of circumstances test to determine the voluntariness of a confession in the criminal context for many years. *See, e.g., Spano v. N.Y.* 360 U.S. 325 (1959).

[242] It is difficult to imagine a bright-line rule that could possibly accommodate all of the various factors considered by the courts when determining the weight of an allegedly involuntary statement.

[243] No. 05-cv-2385, 2009 WL 2149949, at *1 (D.D.C. July 17, 2009). Because the government's case rested almost entirely on Jawad's statements, Judge Huvelle later granted Jawad's petition for habeas corpus. *See Bacha v. Obama*, No. 05-cv-2385, 2009 WL 2365846 (D.D.C. July 30, 2009).

[244] *Anam*, 2010 WL 58965, at *4. These techniques included being suspended in his cell by his left hand and blasting petitioner's cell with music twenty-four hours a day. *Id.*

[245] *Awad v. Obama*, 646 F. Supp. 2d 20, 24 n.2 (D.D.C. 2009).

[246] *Id.*

[247] The language used by the courts that have addressed this issue is surprisingly similar, drawing from the prior district court decision in *United States v. Karake*, 443 F. Supp. 2d 8, 87–88 (D.D.C. 2006). *See, e.g., Anam*, 2010 WL 58965 at *4 (citing *Karake*, 443 F. Supp. 2d at 87); *Al Rabiah v. United States*, 658 F. Supp. 2d 11, 36 (D.D.C. 2009) (citing *Karake*, 443 F. Supp. 2d at 87–88 (D.D.C. 2006)).

[248] *See Al Rabiah*, 658 F. Supp. 2d at 36 ("The legal defect associated with the Government's argument is that it has failed to submit evidence from which the Court could find that the coercion that existed in 2003 had dissipated by 2004."); *Anam*, 2010 WL 58965, at *5 ("[T]he Government failed to establish that Petitioner's twenty-three statements to interrogators are untainted.").

[249] *Anam*, 2010 WL 58965, at *7–8.

[250] *Id.* at *5. On the other hand, Judge Hogan admitted statements given by the detainee at his CSRT and Administrative Review Board hearings, since they were made months and years after his coercive interrogations ended and the circumstances of his later statements indicated he did not fear retaliation. *Id.* at *7–8.

[251] *Al Rabiah*, 658 F. Supp. 2d at 36–38. In *Al Rabiah*, the government argued that the taint from coerced statements in 2003 had dissipated by the time the petitioner repeated the confessions at his CSRT proceedings in 2004. The court rejected this argument because the government failed to provide information about whether Al Rabiah had been interrogated between his 2003 and 2004 statements or whether he continued to have contact with the official responsible for extracting his initial confession. The court found that "the evidence suggest[ed] that there was not a 'clean break' between the coercion and his later statements." *Id.* at 36.

[252] *Al Ginco v. Obama*, 626 F. Supp. 2d 123, 128 (D.D.C. 2009).

[253] *See Hatim v. Obama*, No. 05-cv-1429, 2009 WL 5191429, at *11 (D.D.C. Dec. 15, 2009); *Al Adahi v. Obama*, No. 05-cv-0280, 2009 WL 2584685, at *10 (D.D.C. Aug. 17, 2009); *Khan v. Obama*, 646 F. Supp. 2d 6, 18 (D.D.C. 2009) (refusing to grant petitioner's motion for judgment on the record, but stating that the government would be required to prove the petitioner was a member of [terrorist group] HIG at the time of his capture); *Al Ginco*, 626 F. Supp. 2d at 130.

[254] *Al Ginco*, 626 F. Supp. 2d at 127.

[255] *Id.* at 129.

[256] *Id.*

[257] *Hatim*, 2009 WL 5191429, at *10.

[258] *Al Adahi*, 2009 WL 2584685, at *10.

[259] *Basardh v. Obama*, 612 F. Supp. 2d 30, 35 (D.D.C. 2009).

[260] *Id.* Although portions of the opinion are redacted, Judge Huvelle is likely referring to the fact that Basardh was described in the media as a government informant. *See* Del Quentin Wilber, *Detainee-Informer Presents Quandary for Government*, WASH. POST, Feb. 3, 2009, at A1, *available at*: http://www.washingtonpost.com/wp-dyn/content/article/2009/02/02/AR2009020203337_pf.html.

[261] *Awad v. Obama*, 646 F. Supp. 2d 20, 24 (D.D.C. 2009) (Judge Robertson refused to adopt Judge Huvelle's reasoning in Basardh, stating, "It seems ludicrous to believe that . . . [the petitioner] poses a security threat now, but that is not for me to decide.").

[262] *See, e.g., Ahmed v. Obama*, 613 F. Supp. 2d 51, 55 (D.D.C. 2009).

[263] *Id.* at 55–56.

[264] *El Gharani v. Bush*, 593 F. Supp. 2d 144, 149 (D.D.C. 2009).

[265] *Id.*

[266] *Id.*

[267] *See, e.g., Mohammed v. Obama*, No. 05-cv-1347, 2009 WL 4884194, at *6 (D.D.C. Dec. 16, 2009) ("[T]he mosaic theory is only as persuasive as the tiles which compose it and the glue which binds them together—just as a brick wall is only as strong as the individual bricks which support it and the cement that keeps the bricks in place. Therefore, if the individual pieces of a mosaic are inherently flawed or do not fit together, then the mosaic will split apart, just as the brick wall will collapse."); *Al Adahi v. Obama*, No. 05-cv-0280, 2009 WL 2584685, at *4–5 (D.D.C. Aug. 17, 2009) (same); *Ahmed*, 613 F. Supp. 2d at 55–56 (same).

[268] *Ahmed*, 613 F. Supp. 2d at 56.

[269] *See, e.g., El Gharani*, 593 F. Supp. 2d at 149; *see also Boumediene v. Bush*, 579 F. Supp. 2d 191, 199 (D.D.C. 2008) (ordering the release of five of the six petitioners seeking writ on remand from the Supreme Court).

[270] *In re Guantánamo Bay Detainee Litigation*, 581 F. Supp. 2d 33, 43 (D.D.C. 2008), *rev'd sub nom. Kiyemba v. Obama*, 555 F.3d 1022 (D.C. Cir. 2009).

[271] *See Kiyemba*, 555 F.3d 1022, *cert. granted*, 77 U.S.L.W. 3577, 78 U.S.L.W. 3010, 78 U.S.L.W. 3233, 78 U.S.L.W. 3237 (U.S. Oct. 20, 2009) (No. 08-1234), 130 S. Ct. 458, *vacated*, 78 U.S.L.W. 3492, 78 U.S.L.W. 3497 (U.S. Mar. 1, 2010) (No. 08-1234), 130 S. Ct. 1235.

[272] *Kiyemba v. Obama*, 77 U.S.L.W. 3577, 78 U.S.L.W. 3010, 78 U.S.L.W. 3233, 78 U.S.L.W. 3237 (U.S. Oct. 20, 2009) (No. 08-1234), 130 S. Ct. 458 (mem.).

[273] *See Kiyemba v. Obama*, 78 U.S.L.W. 3492, 78 U.S.L.W. 3497 (U.S. Mar. 1, 2010) (No. 08-1234), 130 S. Ct. 1235 (mem.).

[274] *Id.*

[275] *Kiyemba v. Obama*, 2010 U.S. App. LEXIS 10967 (D.C. Cir. May 28, 2010).

[276] Wittes et al., *supra* note19, at 3, 81.

[277] Respondents' Memorandum Regarding the Government's Detention Authority Relative to Detainees Held at Guantánamo Bay at 2, *In re Guantánamo Bay Detainee Litigation*, 581 F. Supp. 2d 33 (D.D.C. Mar. 13, 2009) (No. 08-cv-442).

[278] Josh Gerstein, *Lindsey Graham: White House Mulling Indefinite Detention*, POLITICO, Feb. 15, 2010, *available at* http://www.politico.com/news/stories/0210/32998.html.

[279] Respondents' Memorandum Regarding the Government's Detention Authority Relative to Detainees Held at Guantánamo Bay at 2, *In re Guantánamo Bay Detainee Litigation*, 581 F. Supp. 2d 33 (D.D.C. Mar. 13, 2009) (No. 08-cv-442) (emphasis added).

www.ingramcontent.com/pod-product-compliance
Lightning Source LLC
Chambersburg PA
CBHW051425200326

41520CB00023B/7366